Intermediate

SECOND EDITION

Select Readings

Teacher-approved readings for today's students

LINDA LEE + ERIK GUNDERSEN

D1501339

OXFORD
UNIVERSITY PRESS

OXFORD
UNIVERSITY PRESS

198 Madison Avenue
New York, NY 10016 USA

Great Clarendon Street, Oxford OX2 6DP UK

Oxford University Press is a department of the University of Oxford.
It furthers the University's objective of excellence in research,
scholarship, and education by publishing worldwide in

Oxford New York

Auckland Cape Town Dar es Salaam Hong Kong Karachi
Kuala Lumpur Madrid Melbourne Mexico City Nairobi
New Delhi Shanghai Taipei Toronto

With offices in

Argentina Austria Brazil Chile Czech Republic France Greece
Guatemala Hungary Italy Japan Poland Portugal Singapore
South Korea Switzerland Thailand Turkey Ukraine Vietnam

OXFORD and OXFORD ENGLISH are registered trademarks of
Oxford University Press in certain countries.

© Oxford University Press 2011

Database right Oxford University Press (maker)

General Manager: Laura Pearson
Editorial Director, International Schools and Adult: Pam Murphy
Associate Editor: Tracey Gibbins
Director, ADP: Susan Sanguily
Executive Design Manager: Maj-Britt Hagsted
Electronic Production Manager: Julie Armstrong
Image Manager: Trisha Masterson
Production Coordinator: Elizabeth Matsumoto
Senior Manufacturing Controller: Eve Wong

ISBN: 978-0-19-433212-5

Printed in China

This book is printed on paper from certified and well-managed sources.

10 9 8 7 6 5 4 3 2 1

ACKNOWLEDGMENTS
Cover photo: hana/Datacraft/Getty Images
*The authors and publisher are grateful to those who have given permission to
reproduce the following extracts and adaptations of copyright material:*
pg. 3 "Answering 6 common interview questions" from CareerBuilder.com, Friday,
December 9, 2005. Copyright © 2005 CareerBuilder, LLC. Reprinted by permission,
www.careerbuilder.com. pg. 9 from "Local Girl Among Finalists for Australian Dream
Job" by Jean Yueh, April 3, 2009 from www.taiwantoday.tw. Reprinted by permission.
pg. 13 from "5 Under 25: Young Women Changing the World" by Jenny Inglee to be
retitled "Young Women Changing the World." Reprinted by permission of the author.
pg. 19 from "Chen Shu-chu, Taiwanese Vegetable Seller, Inspires Others With
Generous Donations to Charity," July 7, 2010 at www.huffingtonpost.com. Reprinted
by permission. pg. 23 from "Getting Ready for the Message" to be titled "Student
Learning Teams" from *Your College Experience*, 9E by John Gardner et al. Copyright
© 2011 by Bedford/St. Martin's. Reproduced by permission of Bedford/St. Martin's.
pg. 33 from "Babies Prove Sound Learners" by Emily Sohn from *Science News for Kids*,
January 16, 2008. Reprinted with permission of Science News. pg. 43 "The Man in the
Moon Has Company" by Alan M. MacRobert from *Boston Globe*, November 18, 1991.
Reprinted by permission of Sky & Telescope Media, LLC. pg. 53 "Culture Shock" by
Bob Weinstein, Editor-in-Chief, Troy Media. Reprinted by permission of the author.
pg. 63 "Private Lives" by Diane Daniel. Reprinted by permission of the author.
www.bydianedaniel.com. pg. 73 "A Young Blind Whiz on Computers" by Lee Berton
from *The Wall Street Journal*, August 15, 1997. Copyright © 1997 Dow Jones & Company,
Inc. Reprinted with permission of Dow Jones & Company, Inc. In the format Textbook
via Copyright Clearance Center. All Rights Reserved Worldwide. pg. 79 "Lilly Gaskin–
Two-Year-Old Geography Whiz" from edwindwianto.wordpress.com. Reprinted by
permission of Edwin Dwianto. pg. 83 "How to Make a Speech" by George Plimpton.
Reprinted by the permission of Russell & Volkening, Inc., as agents for the author.
Copyright © 1985 by George Plimpton. pg. 93 from "Conversational Ball Games" from
Polite Fictions: Why Japanese and Americans Seem Rude to Each Other by Nancy Masterson
Sakamoto. Reprinted with permission of Nancy Masterson Sakamoto. pg. 103 "Letters
of Application" by Andrea B. Geffner from *Business Letters the Easy Way*. Copyright
© 1998 by Barrons Educational Series, Inc. Reprinted by arrangement with Barrons
Educational Series, Inc. pg. 109 "Before, During, and After a Job Interview" by Peggy
Schmidt from *The 90-Minute Interview Prep Book*, 1996. Reprinted by permission of
Peggy Schmidt. newcenturycommunications@gmail.com. pg. 113 "Out to Lunch"
by Joe Robinson. Reprinted by permission of Joe Robinson. pg. 123 "Public Attitudes
Toward Science" from *Black Holes and Baby Universes and Other Essays* by Stephen W.
Hawking. Used by permission of Bantam Books, a division of Random House, Inc., and
Writer's House LLC. pg. 133 from "The Art of Genius: Six Ways to Think Like Einstein"
by Michael Michalko. Originally appeared in the May 1998 issue of *The Futurist*, Used
with the permission of World Future Society. www.wfs.org. pg. 139 "Five Fascinating
Facts about Albert Einstein" by Virginia Calkins. Reprinted by permission of
Cobblestone Magazine, October 1987, © 1987 by Carus Publishing Company.
pg 163 Reproduced by permission of Oxford University Press. From *Oxford American
Dictionary for learners of English* © Oxford University Press 2010.
Realia by: Pronk Media
Maps: Alan Kikuchi
*We would also like to thank the following for permission to reproduce the following
photographs:* D. Hurst / Alamy, back cover (mp3 player); Emmanuel Faure / Iconica /
Getty Images, pg. 1 (business); Robert Kneschke / Shutterstock, pg. 3 (business man);
TORSTEN BLACKWOOD / AFP / Getty Images, pg. 9 (Clare Wang); Gary Cook / Alamy,
pg. 11 (volunteer); Kevin Schafer / Alamy, pg. 14 (West Indian Manatee); Brian Zak
/ Sipa / APImages, pg. 19 (Chen Shu-chu); Monkey Business Images / Shutterstock,
pg. 21 (students); Michael Dwyer / Alamy, pg. 23 (graduates); Gift of Audrey Jones
Beck / Bridgeman Art Library International, pg. 31 (painting); Purdue News Service
photo / David Umberger, pg. 33 (child); Koji Sasahara / AP Photo; pg. 39 (students);
Stockbyte / OUP, pg. 41 (moon); mtkang / Shutterstock, pg. 44 (moon); AP Photo /
Shawn Baldwin, pg. 51 (immigrants); anthonysp / istockphoto.com, pg. 53 (driver);
Andersen Ross / Photodisc / Getty Images, pg. 59 (teenage boy); Bequest of Mrs Mavis
Joan Davis / Bridgeman Art Library International, pg. 61 (painting); Chris Cheadle/
Photographer's Choice / Getty Images, pg. 63 (raft); Wessel Kok, pg. 64 (Diane
Daniel); Tatiana Grozetskaya / Shutterstock, pg. 69 (beach); visi.stock / Shutterstock,
pg. 71 (business man); Gunnar Pippel / Shutterstock, pg. 73 (computer code); Brian
Moore / istockphoto.com, pg. 79 (girl); Inmagine / Alamy, pg. 81 (students); Celia
Peterson / Photolibrary, pg. 83 (student); Bernard Gotfryd / Getty Images, pg. 85
(George Plimpton); Paul Gilham / Getty Images, pg. 91 (tennis court); Global Business
Communication / Getty Images, pg. 93 (business); David Madison / Getty Images,
pg. 99 (volleyball players); Peter Dazeley / Photographer's Choice / Getty Images,
pg. 101 (students); stryjek / Shutterstock, pg. 103 (woman); Christie's Images /
SuperStock , pg. 111 (painting); imagebroker / Alamy, pg. 113 (street restaurant);
Imagesource / Photolibrary, pg. 119 (business meeting); NASA, ESA, C.R. O'Dell
(Vanderbilt University), M. Meixner and P. McCullough (STScI). http://hubblesiteorg/
gallery/album/nebula_collection/pr2004032d/, pg. 121 (Helix Nebula); Chris Pearsall
/ Alamy, pg. 123 (student in lab); Dimitrios Kambouris / Staff / WireImage, pg. 125
(Stephen Hawking); Paul Foreman / Mind Map Inspiration, pg. 131 (DaVinci's Mind
Map); Lebrecht Music and Arts Photo Library / Alamy, pg. 133 (Mozart); Science
Source / Photo Researchers, Inc, pg. 139 (Albert Einstein); Nuri Bilge Ceylan / NBC
films, pg. 140 (Oktay Sinanoglu); Yuri_Arcurs / istockphoto, pg. iii (business woman);
UpperCut Images / Getty Images, pg. iii (man); Fuse / Getty, pg. iii (woman).

Teacher-approved readings for today's students

Teachers tell us that the single most important factor in engaging their students in reading courses is having a book that offers high-interest, level-appropriate content. So, as its title suggests, *Select Readings*, *Second Edition* features dynamic, carefully-selected readings chosen by experienced teachers to meet the needs of today's global learners.

The publisher would like to thank the following teachers who worked closely with us to select and approve the topics and reading passages throughout *Select Readings*, *Second Edition*:

Paul Batt, EMLI, Taichung

Andrew Boon, Toyo Gakuen University, Japan

Crystal Brunelli, Tokyo Jogakkan Middle and High School, Japan

İlke Büyükduman, Istanbul Sehir University, Turkey

Tina Chantal Chen, English Language Institute of Testing and Education, Zhonghe City

Kim Dammers, Konyang University, Korea

Erdogan Erturkoglu, Bezmi Alem University, Turkey

Lee Faire, Toyama College of Foreign Languages, Japan

Yuehchiu Fang, National Formosa University, Huwei

Wendy M. Gough, St. Mary College/Nunoike Gaigo Senmon Gakko, Japan

Michael Griffin, Chung-Ang University, Korea

Hirofumi Hosokawa, Fukuoka Jo Gakuin University, Japan

Zoe Hsu, National Tainan University, Tainan

Cecile Hwang, Changwon National University, Korea

Zeynep Kurular, ITU SFL Prep School, Turkey

Carmella Lieske, Shimane University, Japan

Desiree Lin, Tunghai University, Taichung City

Wan-yun Sophia Liu, CEO Language Institute, Sanchong City

Wen-Hsing Luo, National Hsinchu University of Education, Hukou

Shuji Narita, Osaka University of Economics, Japan

Aybike Oğuz, Özyeğin University, Turkey

Sakae Onoda, Kanda University of International Studies, Japan

Zekariya Özşevik, KTO Karatay University, Turkey

Erick Romero, Centro de Educación Integral de Celaya S.C., Mexico

Jessica Hsiu-ching Shen, Chia Nan University of Pharmacy & Science, Tainan

Mi-Young Song, Kyungwon University International Language Center, Korea

Susan Sunflower, Teacher Education Consultant, U.S.

David Tonetti, Sullivan School, Korea

N J Walters, Kagoshima Immaculate Heart University, Japan

Shan-Shan Wang, National Taiwan University, Taipei

Contents

Scope and Sequence

Chapter	Content	Reading Skill	Building Vocabulary
Chapter 1 Answering 6 Common Interview Questions	Answering interview questions	Using context	Understanding phrasal verbs
Chapter 2 Young Women Changing the World	Making a difference in the world	Making inferences	Understanding suffixes
Chapter 3 Student Learning Teams	Achieving academic success through teamwork	Skimming and Scanning	Learning collocations
Chapter 4 Learning to Speak	How children learn languages	Distinguishing facts from opinions	Understanding connecting words
Chapter 5 The Man in the Moon Has Company	What you can see when you look at the moon	Using context clues	Learning synonyms
Chapter 6 Culture Shock	Adjusting to life in a foreign country	Finding the topic and main idea	Learning collocations
Chapter 7 Private Lives	Having a special place to go to reflect on life	Identifying supporting ideas	Learning noun suffixes

Series Overview
with Teaching Suggestions

Select Readings, *Second Edition* is a reading course for students of English. In *Select Readings*, *Second Edition*, high-interest, authentic reading passages serve as springboards for reading skills development, vocabulary building, and thought-provoking discussions and writing.

The readings represent a wide range of genres (newspaper and magazine articles, personal essays, textbook chapters, book excerpts, and on-line discussions) gathered from well-respected sources, such as *The Wall Street Journal*, the *Utne Reader*, and *Science News*, and approved by experienced teachers.

General Approach to Reading Instruction

The following principles have guided the development of *Select Readings*, *Second Edition*:

- **Exposing students to a variety of text types and genres helps them develop more effective reading skills**. Students learn to handle the richness and depth of writing styles they will encounter as they read more widely in English.

- **Readers become engaged with a selection when they are asked to respond personally to its theme**. While comprehension questions help students see if they have understood the information in a reading, discussion questions ask students to consider the issues raised by the passage.

- **Readers sharpen their reading, vocabulary-building, and language skills when skills work is tied directly to the content and language of each reading passage**. This book introduces students to reading skills such as skimming and scanning and vocabulary-building strategies such as learning synonyms and understanding phrasal verbs. Each skill was chosen in consultation with teachers to ensure that the most applicable and appropriate skills were selected for students at the Intermediate level.

- **Good readers make good writers**. Reading helps students develop writing skills, while writing experience helps students become better readers.

- **Background knowledge plays an important role in reading comprehension**. An important goal of *Select Readings*, *Second Edition* is to illustrate how thinking in advance about the topic of a reading prepares readers to better comprehend and interact with a text.

Chapter Overview

Each chapter in *Select Readings*, *Second Edition* includes the eight sections described below.

1. Opening Page

The purpose of this page is to draw readers into the theme and content of the chapter with relevant artwork and a compelling quotation.

Teaching Suggestions:

- Ask students to describe what they see in the photo(s) or artwork on the page and guess what the chapter is about. Have them read the quotation, restate it in their own words, and then say if they agree with it. Finally, ask what connection there might be between the image and the quotation.

- Call students' attention to the *Chapter Focus* box. Give them a chance to think about the content and skills they are about to study and to set their own learning goals for the chapter.

2. Before You Read

The first activity in each *Before You Read* section is designed to get students to connect personally to the topic of the chapter and to activate their background knowledge of the topic. A second activity or question in this section asks students to further explore their knowledge of the topic by completing a task with a partner. The third activity asks students to complete a *Previewing Chart*, which provides specific tasks for previewing a text. The purpose of this chart is to encourage students to make a habit of using simple previewing strategies before they read any text.

Teaching Suggestions:

- Make sure that students understand the purpose of the *Before You Read* activities. Explain that activating prior knowledge will help them to better comprehend the reading passage.

3. Reading Passage

In general, the readings become increasingly long and/or more complex as the chapters progress. To help students successfully tackle each passage, we have provided the following support tools:

Vocabulary glosses. Challenging words and expressions are glossed throughout the readings. In most cases, we have glossed chunks of words instead of individual vocabulary items. This approach helps students develop a better sense of how important context is to understanding the meaning of new words.

Culture and Language Notes. On pages 141–158, students will find explanations for cultural references and language usage that appear in blue type in the readings. Notes are provided on a wide range of topics from scientific information, to geographical references, to famous people.

Maps. Each location featured in a reading passage is clearly marked on one of the maps found on pages 159–162.

Numbered lines. For easy reference, every fifth line of each reading passage is numbered.

Recorded reading passages. Listening to someone reading a text aloud helps language learners see how words are grouped in meaningful chunks, thus aiding comprehension.

Teaching Suggestions:

- Encourage students to read actively. Circling words, writing questions in the margins, and taking notes are three ways in which students can make reading a more active and meaningful experience.
- Play the recorded version of the reading passage and ask students to listen to how the reader groups words together. As they listen to the recording, students can lightly underline or circle the groups of words.

4. After You Read: Understanding the Text

Following each reading, there are two to three post-reading activities that give students the chance to (a) clarify their understanding of the text, (b) practice reading skills previously introduced, and (c) discuss the issues raised in the reading. The first activity in this section is designed to give students practice with the types of comprehension questions used on exams such as **TOEFL®**, **TOEIC®, and IELTS™**. Questions are also labeled to highlight the reading skill required to answer the question.

Teaching Suggestions:

- Get students to discuss their reactions to the readings in pairs or groups. The process of discussing questions and answers gives students an opportunity to check their comprehension more critically.
- If time permits and you would like students to have additional writing practice, ask them to write a short essay or a journal entry on one of the questions in the *Consider the Issues* section.

5. Building Vocabulary

Reading extensively is an excellent way for students to increase their vocabulary base. Considering this, we pay careful attention to developing students' vocabulary-building skills in each chapter of **Select Readings**, **Second Edition**. A variety of vocabulary-building skills are introduced and recycled throughout the book. Each *Building Vocabulary* section starts out with a short explanation and examples of the skill in focus. In the activities that follow the explanation, students typically scan the reading to gather and analyze various types of words and then use the words in a new context.

Teaching Suggestions:

- View the explanation and examples at the beginning of each *Building Vocabulary* section before asking students to tackle the activities that follow. Encourage them to ask any questions they have about the explanations or examples.
- Encourage students to keep a vocabulary notebook. Present various ways in which students can organize the words in their notebook: by chapter, by topic, by part of speech, etc.

6. Reading Skill

At the beginning of each *Reading Skill* section, students encounter a short explanation of the skill in focus and, when appropriate, an example of how that skill relates to the reading in the chapter. The first task following this explanation asks students to return to the reading to think about and use the new reading skill. The **new *Apply the Reading Skill*** sections then give students the opportunity to apply the strategy to a *new short reading* that is related to the topic of the main reading passage.

Teaching Suggestions:

- Review the explanations and sample sentences at the beginning of each *Reading Skills* section before asking students to tackle the questions that follow. Encourage them to ask any questions they have about the explanations or examples.

- Reflect with students on the ways in which they can apply the reading skills they have learned in each chapter to other reading passages. Then have them apply the new reading skill as they work with the second reading passage in this section.

7. Discussion and Writing

At the end of each chapter, students have an opportunity to talk and write about a variety of issues. The activities in this section provide students with a chance to broaden their views on the topic of the reading and to address more global issues and concerns.

Teaching Suggestions:

- When time permits, let students discuss a question a second time with a different partner or group. This allows them to apply what they learned in their first discussion of the question.

- Choose one or more of the questions in this section as an essay topic for students.

8. Words to Remember

Each chapter ends with a list of *Words to Remember*. All of these words appear on the Oxford 3000™ word list, and many are also highlighted on the Academic Word List. This section provides an efficient means for students to keep track of important new vocabulary by chapter. In addition, the **new *Mini-Dictionary*** on pages 163–172 features carefully crafted definitions of each *Word to Remember* from the new **Oxford American Dictionary for learners of English**, giving students an alphabetical reference of the words and their definitions all in one place.

Additional Resources for Teachers of Reading

- *Teaching Second Language Reading* by Thom Hudson
- *Techniques and Resources in Teaching Reading* by Sandra Silberstein
- *Reading* by Catherine Wallace

Series Components

Testing Program CD-ROM with Student Book Answer Key

Students today are facing increased pressure to excel at standardized testing in order to gain entrance to universities and secure competitive jobs. *Select Readings*, *Second Edition* offers an exciting new Testing Program CD-ROM, including tests modelled after the **IELTS™**, **TOEFL®**, and **TOEIC®** standardized tests, as well as **general achievement and unit tests**. The reading tests included on the new Testing Program CD-ROM with Student Book Answer Key were written and approved by testing experts to ensure a close connection to the widely-used standardized tests above. Each test features a reading passage followed by questions designed to measure comprehension as well as reading- and vocabulary-skill proficiency. All unit tests feature new and different reading passages to test the skills learned in that unit.

Class Audio CDs

Select Readings, *Second Edition* offers Class Audio CDs featuring carefully recorded **audio of all main reading passages** in each level of the series. Giving students the opportunity to listen to a fluent English speaker as they follow along in the text significantly aids comprehension and supports listening and speaking skill development. This is particularly useful for aural learners, who absorb information best through hearing it presented. Each Class Audio CD features a **variety of accents** to expose students to the many sounds of English around the world today.

Audio Download Center

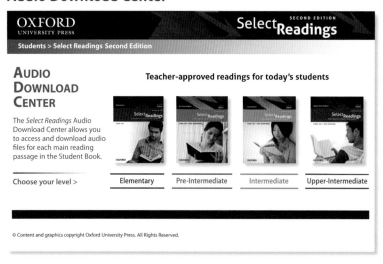

Every main reading from the series is available for **download** through the *Select Readings*, *Second Edition* Audio Download Center. Students and teachers can visit *www.oup.com/elt/selectreadings2e* for access to the downloadable mp3s for any time, anywhere practice and self-study.

*TOEIC® and TOEFL® are registered trademarks of Educational Testing Service (ETS). This publication is not endorsed or approved by ETS.

Answering 6 Common Interview Questions

Chapter Focus

CONTENT
Answering interview questions

READING SKILL
Using context

BUILDING VOCABULARY
Understanding phrasal verbs

"Asking the right questions takes as much skill as giving the right answers."

— Robert Half, American businessman

Before You Read

A. **Connect with the topic.** Have you ever had a job or school interview? How did you prepare for it? What questions were you asked? If you haven't had an interview, what questions do you think an interviewer would ask?

B. **Pair Work.** Which of these common interview questions do you think would be the most difficult to answer? Check (✓) it. Then explain your answer to your partner.

- ☐ Why should we hire you?
- ☐ Why do you want to work here?
- ☐ What are your weaknesses?
- ☐ What did you dislike about your last job?
- ☐ Where do you see yourself five years from now?

C. **Preview the reading.** Look quickly over the article on pages 3–4 to complete the Previewing Chart below.

Previewing Chart

1. Title of the reading: _____

2. Names of people and places in the reading. (List 3 more.)	3. Key words. (What words appear several times? List 5 more.)
Ohio _____	_question_ _____
_____ _____	_____ _____
	_____ _____

4. Read the first sentence in each paragraph. What do you think the reading is probably about?

_____

_____

_____

Answering 6 Common Interview Questions

Copyright CareerBuilder, LLC. Reprinted with permission.

1   While you'll never be able to anticipate every question you might be asked in an interview, you can get a head start[1] by developing strong, concise answers to commonly used questions. Most interviewers will ask similar questions like these to gain knowledge about a candidate's abilities
5   and qualifications and compatibility with[2] the job and the company.

1. Tell me about yourself.

This is often the opening question in an interview. It's also one of the most difficult if you're not prepared. Remember, the interviewer does not want to hear about your hometown or your hobby.

10   This question calls for your one-minute commercial that summarizes your years of experience and skills and your personality in the context of the job for which you are interviewing. Get to the point and sell your professional self. Develop a few brief sentences that demonstrate you have what it takes[3] to do the job—experience, proven results, and
15   desire to contribute.[4]

2. Why should we hire you?

The key to answering any question about you versus your competition is using specifics. "Everybody is going to speak in generalities, so you need something that will make you stand out[5] a bit," said Linda, a teacher in
20   Springfield, Ohio. Give real examples that show them you are best-suited for the job. Linda says she would point out her achievements and accomplishments throughout her career that are relevant[6] to the open position, as well as her experiences in dealing with different types of students and teaching situations. Pinpoint the qualities you have that are
25   truly valuable to the company.

3. Why do you want to work here? What do you know about our company?

Peter, a physician in Indianapolis, said that research is important in answering these questions. "I would use this opportunity to show off what
30   I know about the company and, more importantly, how I would fit in."

🌐 Map page 161

Culture and
Language Notes
page 141

---

[1] **get a head start**   get an early start that gives you an advantage
[2] **compatibility with**   suitability for
[3] **you have what it takes**   you have the skills and abilities
[4] **contribute**   give time and effort
[5] **stand out**   look better than everyone else
[6] **relevant**   related; important

Susan, a vice president of **benefits** in Chicago, said that she would address issues and challenges in the company to demonstrate the depth of her knowledge. "I usually talk about **revenue**, numbers of employees, and also challenges in their type of business and how my experience relates to 35 that," she said. "I would point out things I have done in similar companies that could address their problems."

4. What are your weaknesses?

The secret to answering this question is using your weaknesses to your advantage. "I would turn my weaknesses into strengths," said Tara, an 40 **attorney**. "For example, if my weaknesses include my lack of patience, I would then state that, because of this, I have learned to take special measures[7] to ensure that I remain calm and attentive." Just make sure that you do give a real answer to this question. None of us is without faults, so don't pretend that you do not have weaknesses.

45 5. What did you dislike about your last job? Why did you leave your last job?

You need to be cautious about these kinds of questions and make sure you do not end up sounding bitter.[8] "I would never talk down[9] about my former company, the boss, or my former co-workers," Tara said.

50 You need to have a good understanding about the job for which you're applying to turn this question into a positive one. It may be best to say that you really enjoyed many aspects of your job, then focus on how this new job will give you the opportunity to contribute more in a particular area that is key to the position.

55 6. Where do you see yourself in five years?

An interviewer does not want to hear that your five-year aspiration is to be sailing in the Caribbean or working in a different industry. You need to talk about goals you have that relate to the job. This will demonstrate that you understand the industry and the company and are 60 motivated to succeed there. Susan, the director of public relations at a major car rental company, said she would keep her answer specific to her field, such as stating that she sees herself as **vice president of corporate communications**.

Preparation is the key to answering any question with poise and 65 confidence. Always keep in mind—whatever the question is—that the interviewer is trying to uncover if you are a good fit and can make a positive contribution to the job.

Word Count: 726 | Reading Time: _____ | Words per Minute: _____
(Minutes) | (Word Count/Reading Time)

---

[7] **take special measures**   do specific things
[8] **bitter**   resentful
[9] **talk down**   say negative things

After You Read

Understanding the Text

A. Comprehension

For each item below, fill in the correct circle.

1. **Identifying the Author's Purpose** The purpose of the article is to ____.
   - Ⓐ help job interviewers ask good questions
   - Ⓑ help people answer interview questions well
   - Ⓒ help people identify their job skills
   - Ⓓ show what happens at a job interview

2. **Understanding Pronoun References** In line 7, the word *it* refers to ____.
   - Ⓐ an interview
   - Ⓑ your hometown
   - Ⓒ "Tell me about yourself."
   - Ⓓ the opening question in an interview

3. **Scanning for Details** When you are asked to tell an interviewer about yourself, you should ____.
   - Ⓐ say everything you can think of about your background and interests
   - Ⓑ say a few things that show you can do the job
   - Ⓒ tell the interviewer you can do the job
   - Ⓓ summarize your hobbies and interests

4. **Scanning for Details** If an interviewer asks about your weaknesses, you should ____.
   - Ⓐ identify a weakness and explain how you have learned to deal with it
   - Ⓑ say that you don't have any weaknesses
   - Ⓒ identify an imaginary weakness that isn't very important
   - Ⓓ describe all of your weaknesses in detail

5. **Identifying the Author's Purpose** Why does the author quote different people in the article?
   - Ⓐ The author wants to add humor to the article.
   - Ⓑ The author wants to show what you shouldn't do at a job interview.
   - Ⓒ The author doesn't have enough experience to provide his own examples.
   - Ⓓ The author wants to use specific examples to support the main idea.

B. Identifying Main Ideas and Details

Look back over the reading for details to support each main idea below. Write them in the chart. Several answers are possible.

Question	Main Idea	Details
1. Tell me about yourself.	You should summarize your skills and experience as they relate to the job.	*Don't talk about unrelated things.*
2. Why should we hire you?	You need to give specifics to show you are the best person for the job.	
3. Why do you want to work here? What do you know about our company?	Show what you know about the company and how you would fit in.	
4. What are your weaknesses?	Turn your weaknesses into strengths.	
5. What did you dislike about your last job?	Say something positive about your last job.	
6. Where do you see yourself in five years?	Talk about goals that relate to the company with which you are interviewing.	

C. Consider the Issues

Work with a partner to answer the questions below.

1. In the article on pages 3–4, the author recommends answering interview questions with specific rather than general answers. For each general answer below, think of a more specific answer.

   a. I'm a good student.

   b. I'm easy to work with.

   c. My last boss liked my work.

2. The author says that you should learn about a company before the interview. What are some ways you could do this?

3. Which of the author's tips do you find the most helpful? Why?

Building Vocabulary

Understanding Phrasal Verbs

Phrasal verbs have two or three parts: a verb + one or two other words like *down*, *up*, *off*, or *out*. A phrasal verb has a special meaning which is different from the meaning of the individual words. For example, in the sentence below, the phrasal verb *stand out* means *to be easy to notice*.

"Everybody is going to speak in generalities, so you need something that will make you **stand out** a bit," said Linda.

You can find the meaning of a phrasal verb in a good dictionary.

A. Scan the reading on pages 3–4 to find the missing word in each phrasal verb below. Then match each verb to a definition on the right.

Phrasal Verb	Meaning
1. stand ___*out*___ ___*e*___	**a.** belong
2. talk _____ _____	**b.** result in
3. show _____ _____	**c.** display clearly
4. fit _____ _____	**d.** say negative things about
5. end _____ _____	**e.** be easy to notice

B. Now use the correct form of a phrasal verb from the chart to complete each sentence below.

1. After a lot of discussion about what to do, they _____ staying at home.

2. When you move to a new school, it can take a long time to

_____.

3. It annoys me when someone _____ about my friends.

4. A lot of people have tattoos today. Fifty years ago, people got tattoos because they wanted to _____. Now people get them because they want to fit in.

5. People who are always _____ their expensive clothes can be very irritating.

Reading Skill

Using Context

When you are reading, it is important to use context (the surrounding words and ideas) to guess the meanings of unfamiliar words. You might not be able guess the exact meaning of the word, but you can usually guess its general meaning.

You can often find an <u>example</u> in the context that explains the unfamiliar word. In the sentence below, the two underlined examples help to define the word *aspiration*.

> An interviewer does not want to hear that your five-year **aspiration** is <u>to be sailing in the Caribbean</u> or <u>working in a different industry</u>.

There may also be <u>contrasting information</u> or an <u>explanation</u> in the context that helps you to understand an unfamiliar word, as in the sentences below.

> The key to answering any question about you versus your competition is using **specifics**. "Everybody is going to speak in <u>generalities</u>, so you need <u>something that will make you stand out a bit</u>," said Linda, a teacher in Springfield, Ohio. Give <u>real examples</u> that show them you are best-suited for the job.

A. Analyze the Reading

Read these sentences and answer the questions below.

1. "While you'll never be able to **anticipate** every question you might be asked in an interview, you can get a head start by developing strong, **concise** answers to commonly used questions."

   a. Is *anticipate* a verb, noun, or adjective?

   b. What words in the sentence help you to understand the meaning of the word *anticipate*? What do you think *anticipate* means?

   c. From the context, would you say that a *concise* answer is something good or bad?

2. "This question calls for your one-minute commercial that **summarizes** your years of experience and skills and your personality in the context of the job for which you are interviewing."

   a. Is *summarizes* a verb, noun, or adjective?

   b. What words in the sentence help you to understand the meaning of *summarizes*?

   c. What do you think the word *summarizes* means in this context?

B. Apply the Reading Skill

Read the article below and use context to guess the missing words. (Many different words are possible.)

Local Girl Among Finalists for Australian Dream Job

by Jean Yueh

In 2009, Clare Wang, a young interpreter from Taiwan, won a _____ (1) among the finalists for what has been _____ (2) "the best job in the world"—caretaker of an Australian tropical island. The application process started on January 9 and ended February 22. About 35,000 people, including dancers, scientists, chefs, and students from nearly 200 countries, applied for

the _____ (3). Each applicant had to _____ (4) a video in English no more than one minute long to explain why he or she was the right person for the job.

    Wang, a 30-year-old Chinese-English interpreter, said this was the first time she had campaigned on the Internet. "Usually, I do not take part in this kind of _____ (5)," she told a local newspaper, describing herself as a shy person. In her application video, the young woman used two puppets to _____ (6) her interpreting skills, as well as pictures of herself in leisure-time activities, to _____ (7) online voters she was an outdoor person. Wang ended her video by saying, "I've never been to the Great Barrier Reef, which makes me the perfect explorer." She then _____ (8) that she would be "super curious," as printed on the T-shirt she put on in front of the camera.

Now compare your answers with a partner. Are your words the same? Are they similar?

Discussion & Writing

1. What are some things you probably shouldn't say at a university or job interview? Why?

2. In writing, describe one of your weaknesses. Remember to follow the author's suggestion by turning your weakness into something positive.

   Example

   I used to be a perfectionist about everything, but over the years I have learned that there are times when it is good to demand perfection and times when it is not. Now I am able to evaluate a task and decide how much time and effort to put into it. For important things, I push myself very hard. For less important things, I do what is necessary, but I know when to stop. Learning to do this has helped me in school and in my previous job.

3. Work with a partner to roleplay a job interview. One person is the interviewer and the other is the interviewee. Follow the steps below.

   - Choose a job that sounds interesting to you and your partner and decide what abilities and qualifications are necessary for the job.

   Sample job: an experienced architect for a large architecture firm

   Qualifications: must have ten years experience working in
   a large company
   must be able to work as part of a team
   must have experience designing large office buildings

   - Use the chart you completed on page 6 as you roleplay the job interview.

Mini-Dictionary page 163

Words to Remember		
NOUNS	**VERBS**	**ADJECTIVES**
achievements	anticipate	bitter
aspect	demonstrate	particular
challenges	end up	relevant
confidence	fit in	
contribution	pretend	
opportunity	relate	
patience	show off	
qualifications	stand out	
specifics	talk down	
weakness		

Young Women Changing the World

Chapter Focus

CONTENT
Making a difference in the world

READING SKILL
Making inferences

BUILDING VOCABULARY
Understanding suffixes

"You must be the change you wish to see in the world."

— Mohandas Gandhi (1869–1948)

Before You Read

A. Connect with the topic. Think of two more people who have made a difference in the world in some way. Write about them in the chart below.

Name	What did this person do?
Mohandas Gandhi	He was the leader of the nonviolent movement for independence in India.

B. Pair Work. What do you think are the most serious issues in the world today? Work with a partner to add two or more ideas to the list below. Then check (✓) the issue that concerns you the most.

☐ poverty   ☐ nuclear weapons

☐ pollution   ☐ climate change

☐ _____   ☐ _____

☐ _____   ☐ _____

C. Preview the reading. Look quickly over the article on pages 13–15 to complete the Previewing Chart below.

Previewing Chart

1. Title of the reading: _____

2. Names of people and places in the reading. (List 3 more.)

    <u>Africa</u>   _____

    _____   _____

3. Key words. (What words appear several times? List 3 more.)

    <u>ball</u>   _____

    _____   _____

4. Read the headings and look at the picture. What do you think the reading is probably about?

_____

_____

_____

Young Women Changing the World

by Jenny Inglee

1 *The following article is from the website TakePart. This website gathers news, photos, and videos about today's issues and suggests actions people can take to make a difference. The website also provides stories of people who are working for change locally, nationally, and globally.*

5 **The Soccket Team**
Jessica Lin, Jessica O. Matthews, Julia Silverman, and Hemali Thakkar
Issue: Renewable Energy

In most African countries more than 90 percent of the population lives without electricity. And if you've been to **Africa**, you know that almost
10 that many people play **soccer** whenever they get the chance. But it took four young women to realize that all the energy being used on the field could be used to power people's homes.

The magic soccer ball created by Harvard students Jessica Lin, Jessica Matthews, Julia Silverman, and Hemali Thakkar is beautiful in its
15 simplicity. The "sOccket" captures energy from kick, dribble, and throw, and stores it for later use. Kids can play a game, then bring the ball home and charge an LED lamp, cell phone, or battery. They no longer need to use unhealthy and expensive kerosene lamps or walk three hours to charge their cell phones. And down the line,[1] the founders hope
20 the sOccket will move beyond single-family homes to power hospitals and schools. But think of the immediate impact the ball can have on individual kids: money is saved, families can afford to send their children to school, child labor decreases, and a better world emerges.

Carmina Mancenon
25 Founder, Stitch Tomorrow
Issue: Impoverished Youth

Through Stitch Tomorrow, a youth-led microfinance initiative[2] in the **Philippines** and **Indonesia**, Carmina Mancenon, a 16-year-old from Tokyo, Japan, is empowering underprivileged girls by helping them create
30 fashion lines out of secondhand materials.[3]

Maps
pages 159–162

Culture and
Language Notes
page 142

---

[1] **down the line**   later
[2] **microfinance initiative**   a program that provides loans to people living in poverty, usually to start their own businesses
[3] **secondhand materials**   materials used before

13

Stitch Tomorrow provides fashion and business education, capital,[4] and resources to help the girls turn their clothing design ideas into a reality. Experts are on hand to help the young designers refine their concepts, create partnerships, find sponsors, and show their fashion
35 lines on the runway. This year, Mancenon brought her idea for Stitch Tomorrow to the **World Economic Forum** in Davos, Switzerland. As the youngest participant, she shared her hope for using fashion to bridge the gap[5] between privileged and underprivileged youth around the world.

Stephanie Cohen
40 Founder, Kids Make a Difference
Issue: Endangered Manatees

In second grade, Stephanie Cohen read an article about a baby manatee injured by a boat's propeller as it came up for air—an accident that claims the lives of many manatees every year. An article like that
45 would affect most 8-year-olds. But how many would dedicate their lives to the issue? At least one.

From that day forward, Cohen dedicated herself to raising awareness in her school and community about manatees, eventually starting a foundation called Kids Make a Difference. The organization brings
50 youth together to fundraise for the preservation of wildlife and inspires volunteers to help animals around the world.

Maggie Doyne
Founder, The Blink Now Foundation
Issue: World Poverty

55 Trekking through the Himalayas after high school, Maggie Doyne met hundreds of orphaned and poverty-stricken Nepalese children. They stuck with her. Upon returning to her hometown of Mendham, New Jersey, she asked her community to help her build a safe and loving home for these children.

60 To Doyne's surprise, her neighbors supported the idea. With their help, Doyne and the local Nepalese community built the Kopila Valley Children's Home, a home that provides young orphans, street children, child laborers, and abused children with an education, health care, and a loving place to grow up. Today, there are 25 children living in the home,
65 and 60 children are enrolled in school through the Kopila Outreach program.

---

[4] **capital**   money or supplies invested in a business to make it profitable
[5] **bridge the gap**   lessen the difference

These young women prove that no matter how young you are, if you're passionate about a cause and take action, you're old enough to make a difference.

Word Count: 663 | Reading Time: _____ | Words per Minute: _____
(Minutes) | (Word Count/Reading Time)

After You Read
Understanding the Text

A. Comprehension
For each item below, fill in the correct circle.

1. **Finding the Main Idea** Which of these sentences best expresses the main idea of the article?
   (A) It's not easy to make a difference in the world.
   (B) Young people can make a difference in the world.
   (C) There are many different ways to change the world.
   (D) Young people need to spend time raising money for children.

2. **Understanding Pronoun References** In line 16, the word *it* refers to _____.
   (A) the sOccket
   (B) energy
   (C) kick, dribble, and throw
   (D) the Harvard students

3. **Scanning for Details** Which of the following statements about the sOccket is not true?
   (A) It can save people time.
   (B) It can provide electricity.
   (C) It can save people money.
   (D) It is used in hospitals.

4. **Scanning for Details** Stitch Tomorrow helps young women _____.
   (A) start a career in the fashion industry
   (B) buy their own clothes
   (C) become fashion models
   (D) travel to Europe to learn about fashion

5. Scanning for Details Unlike Maggie Doyne and Carmina Mancenon, Stephanie Cohen dedicated herself to helping ____.

(A) young women

(B) animals

(C) orphans

(D) kids

B. Vocabulary: Using Context

Use context to guess the meaning of each boldfaced word below.

1. The sOccket captures energy from kick, dribble, and throw, and **stores** it for later use.

(A) loses   (C) shares

(B) holds   (D) designs

2. But think of the immediate **impact** the ball can have on individual kids: money is saved, families can afford to send their children to school, child labor decreases, and a better world emerges.

(A) noise   (C) use

(B) fun   (D) effect

3. Experts are **on hand** to help the young designers refine their concepts, create partnerships, find sponsors, and show their fashion lines on the runway.

(A) available   (C) unnecessary

(B) useless   (D) important

4. From that day forward, Cohen dedicated herself to raising awareness in her school and community about manatees, eventually starting a **foundation** called Kids Make a Difference.

(A) game   (C) solution

(B) organization   (D) dedication

C. Consider the Issues

Work with a partner to answer the questions below.

1. In what ways are the young people in this article similar? In what ways are they different?

2. Which of these people do you find the most inspiring? Why?

3. Consider the four issues in the article. Which one do you feel most strongly about? Why? What are some other ways to deal with this issue?

Building Vocabulary

> **Understanding Suffixes**
>
> Understanding suffixes can help you improve your reading comprehension. These special endings on words help you to know if a word is a noun, verb, adjective, or adverb.
>
> For example, the suffix –*tion* at the end of the word *educa<u>tion</u>* signals that it is a noun. The suffix –*ive* at the end of the word *expens<u>ive</u>* signals that it might be an adjective.

A. Scan the reading on pages 13–15 to find words that end in the suffixes below. (Try to find a word for each blank.) Then decide if the words are nouns or adjectives.

-ity	-ness	-tion	-ship	-ful
<u>electricity</u>	<u>business</u>	<u>education</u>	<u>leadership</u>	<u>successful</u>
_____	_____	_____	_____	_____
_____		_____		
_____		_____		
		_____		
		_____		

B. Choose a word from the chart above to complete these sentences. (More than one word may be possible.)

1. As the world's _____ increases, access to clean water and food decreases.

2. It's not easy to take _____ when you see a problem.

3. It's hard to say what the most _____ place in the world is.

4. If _____ is important to you, you don't need to have a lot of possessions.

5. There has to be an _____ of a problem before it can be solved.

6. Learning to read and write is part of a good _____.

7. In the future, some people hope to use _____ to power all cars.

8. If you want to be a professor, you will have to work hard to make your dream become a _____.

Reading Skill

Making Inferences
An inference is a logical conclusion drawn from evidence.

Evidence	**Possible Inferences**
Your friend is crying.	*Your friend is sad.*
	Your friend just got some bad news.

Evidence	**Possible Inferences**
Your friend is in the hospital.	*Your friend is not well.*
	Your friend had an accident.

Readers make inferences as they read a text. They look at the facts or evidence in the text and draw conclusions.

A. Analyze the Reading

What can you infer from these sentences from the reading? Circle the correct word(s) in parentheses to complete the inferences.

1. "In most African countries more than 90 percent of the population lives without electricity. And if you've been to Africa, you know that almost that many people play soccer whenever they get the chance."

   Inference: You can infer that soccer (is / isn't) very popular in Africa.

2. "Kids can play a game, then bring the ball home and charge an LED lamp, cell phone, or battery. They no longer need to use unhealthy and expensive kerosene lamps or walk three hours to charge their cell phones."

   Inference: You can infer that an LED lamp is (more expensive / healthier) than a kerosene lamp.

3. "In second grade, Stephanie Cohen read an article about a baby manatee injured by a boat's propeller as it came up for air—an accident that claims the lives of many manatees every year. An article like that would affect most 8-year-olds. But how many would dedicate their lives to the issue? At least one."

   Inference: You can infer that Stephanie Cohen is a (passionate / creative) person.

B. Apply the Reading Skill

Read the article and then answer the questions in the chart below.

Chen Shu-chu, Taiwanese Vegetable Seller,
Inspires Others with Generous Donations to Charity

Over her lifetime, Chen Shu-chu, a Taiwanese woman who makes a modest[6] living selling vegetables, has donated over NT$10 million to charity (the equivalent of over $300,000 in U.S. currency). Chen accumulated the money working long 18-hour days at a local market and living frugally.

For her amazing contributions to local libraries and orphanages, *TIME* magazine named Chen one of the most influential people of 2010. Now AFP reports that Chen's generous giving has set off a nationwide trend, encouraging others of small means[7] to donate to charity. "The point of Chen's story is that all of a sudden many people found that even though they may not be rich, their tiny but persistent small donations may come as a great help to some people," said Hu Yu-fang of United Way.

Police say they arrested the couple on Sept. 19 after they were allegedly spotted stealing property during an open

What does the article say about Chen Shu-chu? What are the facts?	What can you infer from the facts?
She doesn't earn a lot of money, yet she has given a lot of money to charity.	*She is very generous.*
She has given money to orphanages and libraries.	
TIME magazine named her one of the most influential people of 2010.	

---

[6] **modest** limited
[7] **of small means** who don't earn a lot of money

Discussion & Writing

1. What do these proverbs mean to you? How does each one relate to the ideas in the reading?

   "Talk does not cook rice."
   —Chinese proverb

   "Vision without action is a daydream. Action without vision is a nightmare."
   —Japanese proverb

   "The generous and bold have the best lives."
   —Norwegian proverb

2. Think of someone who has inspired you in some way. Write a paragraph describing this person and then share your paragraph with your classmates.

   Example

   You don't have to do grand things to inspire other people. My aunt inspires me every day simply by the way she deals with problems. Whenever something negative happens to my aunt, she finds a way to laugh about it. She never lets bad things upset her or make her angry. I am always inspired by her ability to do this.

Mini-Dictionary
page 163

Words to Remember

NOUNS	VERBS	ADJECTIVES
capital	abuse	immediate
foundation	(take) action	individual
impact	charge	local
initiative	create	
issue	(make a) difference	
reality	emerge	
resources	realize	
simplicity	suggest	
	support	

Student Learning Teams

CONTENT
Achieving academic success
through teamwork

READING SKILL
Skimming and Scanning

BUILDING VOCABULARY
Learning collocations

"It's in supporting one another that two
hands find strength."

— Abdiliaahi Muuse, Somali sage (1890–1966)

Before You Read

A. **Connect with the topic.** Read the definition of a team below. Then match each team on the left side of the chart with a goal on the right side.

"A team is a small number of people with complementary skills[1] who are committed to a common purpose, set of goals, and approach."
—from the *Harvard Business Review*

Teams	Goals
____ **1.** World Cup team	**a.** to save the lives of patients
____ **2.** software production team	**b.** to develop computer applications
____ **3.** team of doctors in an emergency room	**c.** to find and help lost or injured climbers
____ **4.** search and rescue team in the mountains	**d.** to compete in and win the soccer championship

B. **Pair work.** What makes a team successful? Why are some teams more successful than others? Can you think of examples of successful teams in your country? Share ideas with a partner.

C. **Preview the reading.** Look quickly over the article on pages 23–25 to complete the Previewing Chart below.

Previewing Chart

1. Title of the reading: _____

2. Headings. What headings or subtitles appear in the reading? (List 1 more.)

Activities for a Learning Team

_____

3. Key words. (What words appear several times? List 3 more.)

students _____

_____ _____

4. I think this reading is probably about

_____

_____

_____.

---

[1] **complementary skills**   different abilities that strengthen the team

Student Learning Teams

by John N. Gardner and A. Jerome Jewler
from *Your College Experience*

1   Research has shown that college students can learn as much, or more, from peers[2] as they do from instructors and textbooks. When students work effectively in a supportive group, the experience can be a very powerful way to improve academic achievement and satisfaction with
5 the learning experience.

    Recent interviews with college students at **Harvard University** revealed that nearly every **senior** who had been part of a study group considered this experience crucial to his or her academic progress and success. The list below describes several important activities that you and your study
10 group or **learning team** can collaborate on:

Activities for a Learning Team

    1. Sharing class notes. Team up with[3] other students immediately after class to share and compare notes. One of your teammates may have picked up[4] something you missed or vice versa.[5]

15   **2. Comparing ideas about assigned readings.** After completing each week's readings, team up with other students to compare your **highlighting and margin notes**. See if you all agree on what the author's major points were and what information in the chapter you should study for exams.

20   **3. Doing library research.** Studies show that many students are unfamiliar with library research and sometimes experience "library anxiety." Forming library research teams is an effective way to develop a social support group for reducing this fear and for locating and sharing information.

25   **4. Meeting with the instructor.** Having your team visit the instructor during **office hours** to seek additional assistance in preparing for exams is an effective team learning strategy for several reasons. If you are shy or unassertive, it may be easier to see an instructor in the company of other students. Your team visit also sends a message to the instructor
30   that you are serious about learning.

 Map page 161

Culture and
Language Notes
page 143

---

[2] **peers**   classmates
[3] **team up with**   get together with
[4] **picked up**   understood
[5] **vice versa**   just the opposite, i.e., you may have picked up something your teammates missed

5. Reviewing test results. After receiving test results, the members of a learning team can review their individual tests together to help one another identify the sources of their mistakes and to identify any "model" answers that received maximum credit. You can use this information to improve your performance on subsequent tests or assignments.

Not all learning teams, however, are equally effective. Sometimes group work is unsuccessful or fails to reach its full potential because insufficient thought was given to how teams should be formed or how they should function. The following suggestions are strategies for maximizing the power of peer collaboration:

Strategies for Making a Learning Team Successful

1. In forming teams, seek peers who will contribute quality and diversity. Look for fellow students who are motivated: who attend class regularly, are attentive and participate actively while in class, and complete assignments on time.

Include teammates from both genders as well as students with different personality characteristics. Such variety will bring different life experiences and different styles of thinking and learning strategies to your team, which can increase both its quality and versatility.

Furthermore, choosing only your friends or classmates who have similar interests and lifestyles can often result in a learning group that is more likely to get off track[6] and onto topics that have nothing to do with the learning task.

2. Keep your group size small (three to six classmates). Smaller groups allow for more face-to-face interaction and eye contact and less opportunity for any one individual to shirk his or her responsibility.[7] Also, it's much easier for small groups to get together outside of class.

Consider choosing an even number of teammates so you can work in pairs in case the team decides to divide its work into separate parts for different members to work on.

---

[6] **get off track**   become distracted or lose focus
[7] **shirk his or her responsibility**   not do the work he or she agreed to do

3. **Hold individual team members accountable for**[8] **contributing to the learning of their teammates**. Research on study groups at Harvard University indicates that they are effective only if each member has done the required course work in advance of the group meeting. One way to ensure proper preparation is to ask each member to come to the group meeting prepared with specific information to share with teammates, as well as with questions on which they would like to receive help from the team.

Another way to ensure that each teammate prepares properly for the meeting is to have individual members take on different roles or responsibilities. For example, each member could assume special responsibility for mastering a particular topic,[9] section, or skill to be taught to the others.

This course may be the perfect place for you to form learning teams and to start putting principles of good teamwork into practice.[10] The teamwork skills you build in this course can be applied to your future courses, particularly those which you find most difficult. What's more, **national surveys** of employers consistently show that being able to work effectively in teams is one of the most important and valued skills in today's work world.

Word Count: 798 | Reading Time: _____ (Minutes) | Words per Minute: _____ (Word Count/Reading Time)

About the Authors

John N. Gardner is a professor of library and information science, and A. Jerome Jewler is a professor of journalism and mass communications at the University of South Carolina, Columbia. The authors specialize in helping students make a successful transition from high school to college.

---

[8] **hold someone accountable for**   make someone responsible for
[9] **mastering a particular topic**   becoming an expert in a specific subject area
[10] **putting principles into practice**   incorporating ideas and words into real-life actions

After You Read

Understanding the Text

A. Comprehension

Read the sentences below and write *T* (True), *F* (False), or *I* (Impossible to Know) based on the information in the reading.

_____ **1.** One of the main purposes of the reading is to encourage students to form learning teams.

_____ **2.** In a recent study, virtually all Harvard University students said that joining a study team helped them be more successful.

_____ **3.** According to the reading, a team that includes men and women will probably be more effective than a team with only men.

_____ **4.** To be successful, learning teams need a strong leader.

_____ **5.** It's a good idea to form teams of people who have similar interests.

_____ **6.** You can infer that a team of five people is better than a team of six.

B. Vocabulary: Word Forms

Scan the reading on pages 23–25 to find the missing word forms in the chart below.

Nouns	Verbs	Adjectives
1. support	support	_____ (paragraph 1)
2. _____ (paragraph 8)	_____ (paragraph 2)	collaborative
3. _____ (paragraph 2)	succeed	_____ (paragraph 8)
4. _____ (paragraph 12)	interact	interactive
5. specifics	specify	_____ (paragraph 14)
6. _____ (paragraph 10)	vary	various

C. Consider the Issues

Work with a partner to answer the questions below.

1. The authors describe several learning team activities that can improve your academic performance. Which team activity would help you most? Which activity would help you least? Why?

2. The reading provides information on what you *should* do to form and maintain an effective study team. Make a list of three to five things you *shouldn't* do when putting together and maintaining a learning team.

3. The authors say that teamwork is one of the most valued skills in today's work world. Do you agree? Why or why not?

Building Vocabulary

Learning Collocations

A collocation is two or more words that are often used together.
For example, we use the verb *shirk* most frequently with the nouns
responsibility, *duty*, or *obligations*. We don't use this verb with very many
other nouns.

When you are learning new words, it is helpful to learn the words that go
with them.

A. Scan the reading on pages 23–25 to complete the collocations below. Write
the missing words on the lines.

adjective + noun		adjective + noun		verb + noun	
academic	*achievement*	learning	*experience*	share	*class notes*
	_____		_____		_____
	_____		_____		

B. Use collocations from this page to complete the sentences below. More
than one answer may be possible.

1. A new study suggests that school friends may play a major role in
a teenager's _____ _____.

2. Spending a year at a school in another country is a great _____
_____ for any student.

3. Children often _____ _____ for doing chores around
the house.

4. In the movie, the selfish adults seem to _____ _____ for
their children, who are left to take care of themselves.

5. Many people want to join a _____ _____ to improve their
test scores.

6. There is now a website that allows college students to _____
_____ with others who miss class.

7. She received a scholarship to university due to her _____
_____ in school.

8. Notetaking is an effective _____ _____.

Reading Skill

Skimming and Scanning

Skimming and scanning are techniques for getting different kinds of information from a reading passage. We *skim* a text to get a *general idea* about the text. We *scan* a text to find *specific information* in a text.

Skimming	Scanning
Purpose: • to get a general idea about the text • to find out what the text is about • to identify the main ideas in the text	**Purpose:** • to find a specific fact • to find a specific word • to answer a specific question
How to do it: • Don't read every word. Let your eyes "skim" quickly over the text. • Read the title and subheadings. • Read the introduction or first paragraph. • Read the first and last sentence of each paragraph. • Read the last paragraph.	**How to do it:** • Think about the likely form of the answer to the question. Will it be a number, a date, a person's name? • Ask yourself the question repeatedly as you move your eyes quickly over the text. • Move your eyes quickly over several lines at a time.

A. Analyze the Reading Skill

Read each question below. Then decide if you should skim the text or scan the text for the information. Check (✓) your answers.

	Skim	Scan
1. Does the article have the information I need?	☐	☐
2. What is the article about?	☐	☐
3. How is the article organized?	☐	☐
4. What does the word *concepts* mean?	☐	☐
5. What does the author say about asking questions?	☐	☐
6. Who is the audience for this reading?	☐	☐

B. Apply the Reading Skill

Skim the reading below to answer the appropriate questions from Activity A. Then scan the reading to answer the remaining questions.

Getting Ready for the Message
from *Your College Experience*

Listening in class is not like listening to a TV program, listening to a friend, or even listening to a speaker at a meeting. The difference, of course, is that what is said in class is vital to your success in the class. Knowing how to listen can help you get more out of what you hear, understand better what you have heard, and save you time in the process.

Here are eight strategies that will help you be a more effective listener in class:

1. **Be ready for the message.** Prepare yourself to hear, to listen, and to receive the message.

2. **Listen to the main concepts and central ideas**, not just to facts and figures. Although facts are important, they will be easier to remember when you place them in a context of concepts, themes, and ideas.

3. **Listen for new ideas.** Even if you are an expert on the topic, you can still learn something new. Assuming you have "already heard all this before" means that your mind will be closed to any new information.

4. **Really hear what is said.** Hearing "sounds" is not the same as hearing the intended message. Listening involves hearing what the speaker wants you to receive, to understand, and to learn.

5. **Repeat mentally.** Words that you hear can go in one ear and out the other unless you make an effort to retain them. Think about what you hear and make an active effort to retain it by repeating it silently to yourself.

6. **Think.** Decide whether you think what you have heard is important. Reflect on the new information.

7. **Ask questions.** If you did not hear or understand what was said, raise your hand! Now is the time to clarify things. Typically, one student will ask a question that many students in the room are wondering about.

8. **Sort, organize, and categorize.** When you listen, try to match what you are hearing with your previous knowledge. Take an active role in deciding how you want to recall what you are learning.

C. Evaluate the Reading Skill

Share your answers to the questions in Activity A with a partner. How can skimming and scanning help you become a more effective reader?

Discussion & Writing

1. **Pair Work.** What does the proverb below mean to you? How does it relate to ideas in this chapter?

   "When spiders unite, they can tie up a lion."
   —Ethiopian proverb

2. Forming a student learning team is one effective way to improve your academic performance. What are some other things you can do to be more successful academically? Add two more ideas to the list below. Then choose one idea and write a paragraph explaining to your classmates why you think it is a good way to improve your academic performance.

   Ways to improve your academic performance

   - take notes in class
   - be prepared for every class
   - find a good place to study
   - _____

   - schedule your time carefully
   - improve your memory
   - study actively
   - _____

   Example

   > One way to improve your academic performance is to be prepared for every class. The best way to be prepared for a class is to know a little about the topic before the class begins. You can do this by reading ahead in your textbook or by doing some research online. For example, if you know that the topic of your next history class is going to be the last election, you can read about the subject before class.

3. Form a learning team in this class with a small group of students. Follow as many of the suggestions in this chapter as possible. After one month, tell your classmates about the advantages and disadvantages of working on a learning team.

Mini-Dictionary
page 163

Words to Remember		
NOUNS	**VERBS**	**ADJECTIVES**
anxiety	consider	crucial
experience	ensure	effective
performance	function	proper
potential	reveal	sufficient
responsibility	share	
satisfaction		
source		
strategy		
success		
variety		

Learning to Speak

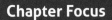

CONTENT
How children learn languages

READING SKILL
Distinguishing facts from opinions

BUILDING VOCABULARY
Understanding connecting words

"Learning never exhausts the mind."

— Leonardo da Vinci, Italian artist and
scientist (1452–1519)

Before You Read

A. Connect with the topic. Do you think these statements about languages and language learning are true or false? Check (✓) your ideas.

	True	False
1. Middle school is the best time to begin learning a new language.	☐	☐
2. Watching television is a good way for a baby to learn a language.	☐	☐
3. It is confusing for a child to learn two languages at the same time.	☐	☐
4. Scientists can't explain how people learn their first language.	☐	☐
5. All languages have the same number of sounds.	☐	☐

B. Pair work. Compare answers with a partner. How many of your answers are the same?

C. Preview the reading. Skim the article on pages 33–35 to complete the Previewing Chart below.

Previewing Chart

1. Title of the reading: _____

2. Names of people and places in the reading. (List 2 more.)

   University of Washington's Institute
   for Learning and Brain Sciences

   _____

   _____

3. Key words. (What words appear several times? List 5 more.)

   research   _____

   _____   _____

   _____   _____

4. Read the headings and the first sentence in each paragraph. What do you think the reading is probably about?

   _____

   _____

   _____

Babies Prove Sound Learners

by Emily Sohn
from *Science News*

1   It can be hard to know what newborns want. They
can't talk, walk, or even point at what they're thinking
about. Yet babies begin to develop language skills
long before they begin speaking, according to recent
5   research. And, compared to adults, they develop these
skills quickly. People have a tough time learning new
languages as they grow older, but infants have the
ability to learn any language, even fake[1] ones, easily.

For a long time scientists have struggled to
10   explain how such young children can learn the
complicated grammatical rules and sounds required
to communicate in words. Now, researchers are
getting a better idea of what's happening in the brains
of society's tiniest language learners. The insights might eventually help
15   kids with **learning disabilities** as well as adults who want to learn new
languages. The work might even help scientists who are trying to design
computers that can communicate like people do. "The brain of the baby
is a new frontier,"[2] says Patricia Kuhl, co-director of the University of
Washington's **Institute for Learning and Brain Sciences**.

20   **The Learning Process**
For decades scientists have debated how the brains of young children
figure out how to communicate using language. With help from new
technologies and research strategies, scientists are now finding that babies
begin life with the ability to learn any language. By interacting with other
25   people and using their superb listening and watching skills, they quickly
master the specific languages they hear most often.

"The [baby] brain is really flexible," says Rebecca Gomez, an
experimental psychologist at the University of Arizona, Tucson. Babies
"can't say much, but they're learning a lot." Kuhl's research, for example,
30   suggests that the progression from babbles like "gaga" to actual words
like "good morning" begins with the ability to tell the difference between
simple sounds, such as "ga," "ba," and "da." Such studies show that, up to

Culture and
Language Notes
page 144

---

[1] **fake**   not real
[2] **a new frontier**   an unexplored area

about six months of age, babies can recognize all the sounds that make up all the languages in the world. "Their ability to do that shows that [babies] are prepared to learn any language," Kuhl says. "That's why we call them 'citizens of the world.'"

About 6,000 sounds make up the languages spoken around the globe, but not every language uses every sound. For example, while the Swedish language distinguishes among 16 vowel sounds, English uses only eight vowel sounds, and Japanese uses just five. Adults can hear only the sounds used in the languages they speak fluently. To a native Japanese speaker, for instance, the letters "R" and "L" sound identical. So, unlike someone whose native language is English, a Japanese speaker cannot tell "row" from "low" or "rake" from "lake."

Starting at around six months old, Kuhl says, a baby's brain focuses on the most common sounds it hears. Then, children begin responding only to the sounds of the language they hear the most. In a similar way, Gomez has found, slightly older babies start recognizing the patterns that make up the rules of their native language. In English, for example, kids who are about 18 months old start to figure out that words ending in "-ing" or "-ed" are usually verbs, and that verbs are action words.

Language on the Brain

Scientists are particularly interested in the brains of people who speak more than one language fluently because that skill is hard to acquire after about age seven. In one of Kuhl's studies, for example, native Mandarin Chinese speakers spoke Chinese to nine-month-old American babies for twelve sessions over four weeks. Each session lasted about 25 minutes. At the end of the study, the American babies responded to Mandarin sounds just as well as did Chinese babies who had been hearing the language their entire lives. (English-speaking teenagers and adults would not perform nearly as well.)

If a child regularly hears two languages, her brain forms a different pathway for each language. However, once the brain solidifies those **electrical language pathways** by around age seven, it gets harder to form new ones. By then, a baby's brain has disposed of,[3] or pruned, all the unnecessary connections that the infant was born with. So, if you don't start studying Spanish or Russian until middle school, you must struggle against years of brain development, and progress can be frustrating. A twelve-year-old's brain has to work much harder to forge language connections than an infant's brain does. "We ought to be learning new languages between ages zero and seven, when the brain does it naturally," Kuhl says.

---

[3] **disposed of**   gotten rid of

Learning from the Baby Brain

For teenagers and adults who want to learn new languages, baby studies
75 may offer some useful tips. For one thing, researchers have found that
it is far better for a language learner to talk with people who speak the
language than to rely on educational CDs and DVDs with recorded
conversations. When infants watched someone speaking a foreign
language on TV, Kuhl found, they had a completely different experience
80 than they did if they watched the same speaker in real life. With real
speakers, the babies' brains lit up with electrical activity when they heard
the sounds they had learned. "The babies were looking at the TV, and they
seemed mesmerized,"[4] Kuhl says. Learning, however, did not happen.
"There was nothing going on in their brains," she says. "Absolutely
85 nothing."

Word Count: 883   Reading Time: _____   Words per Minute: _____
                    (Minutes)   (Word Count/Reading Time)

After You Read
Understanding the Text

A. Comprehension
For each item below, fill in the correct circle.

1. **Scanning for Details** Patricia Kuhl calls babies "citizens of the world"
   because ____.
   (A) all babies are alike
   (B) we are beginning to learn more about the brains of babies
   (C) babies can hear the sounds of all languages
   (D) babies can tell the difference between simple sounds and actual words

2. **Scanning for Details** According to the reading, which of the following
   statements is not true about babies?
   (A) They have the ability to learn any language.
   (B) Their brains create a different pathway for each language they hear.
   (C) They learn languages by listening to and watching people.
   (D) By the time they are nine months old, they can no longer hear the
       sounds of all languages.

---

4 **mesmerized** hypnotized; fascinated

3. **Understanding Pronoun References** The word *they* in line 25 refers to ____.
   Ⓐ skills   Ⓑ languages   Ⓒ people   Ⓓ babies

4. **Using Context** The verb *figure out* in line 22 is closest in meaning to ____.
   Ⓐ learn   Ⓑ forget   Ⓒ explain   Ⓓ help

5. **Using Context** The word *forge* in line 69 is closest in meaning to ____.
   Ⓐ recognize   Ⓑ study   Ⓒ make   Ⓓ require

6. **Making Inferences** It may be concluded that a native English speaker would have trouble learning Swedish because ____.
   Ⓐ English has more vowel sounds than Swedish
   Ⓑ he or she wouldn't be able to hear all of the vowel sounds in Swedish
   Ⓒ the vowel sounds in Swedish would all sound the same
   Ⓓ all of the vowel sounds in Swedish would sound unfamiliar

B. Vocabulary: Word Forms
Look back over the reading to find the missing word forms in the chart below.

Noun	Verb	Adjective
1. flexibility	flex	
2. development		developmental
3.	differ	
4. response		responsive
5. grammar		
6. experiment	experiment	
7.	connect	connected

C. Consider the Issues
Work with a partner to answer the questions below.

1. What did you learn about the brains of babies from the article? List 3 facts.

2. In what order do these events happen in the lives of babies? Number them from 1 to 4.
   ____ They start to recognize grammatical patterns in the languages they hear.
   ____ The brain solidifies the language pathways in the brain.
   ____ They can recognize all the sounds in all the languages in the world.
   ____ Their brains start to focus on the most common sounds they hear.

3. Some parents play foreign language CDs to their young children. Based on the information in this reading, do you think this is useful?

Building Vocabulary

Understanding Connecting Words

Writers use special words and phrases to connect ideas in a text. For the reader, these words are like signposts; they signal the type of information that is coming next. In this way, connecting words help the reader to follow the writer's ideas.

Connecting Words	Purpose	Example
for example for instance like such as for one thing	signals that an example is coming next	Adults can hear only the sounds used in the languages they speak fluently. To a native Japanese speaker, **for instance**, the letters "R" and "L" sound identical.
however yet but	signals that the next sentence contrasts with what came before	They can't talk, walk, or even point at what they are thinking about. **Yet** babies begin to develop language skills long before they begin speaking.
so	signals the result of something mentioned before	By age seven, a child has disposed of all the unnecessary connections that it was born with. **So**, if you don't start studying Spanish until middle school, it will be harder to learn it.

A. Complete each sentence below with the correct connecting word.

1. The Japanese language has only five vowel sounds, _____ the Swedish language has 16. (so / but)

2. Children start to figure out the grammar of a language by the age of two. _____, an English-speaking child may understand that verbs are action words. (however / for instance)

3. Babies can hear the sounds of all languages in the world, _____ they are prepared to learn any language. (so / for example)

4. When babies were watching someone speaking a foreign language on TV, they seemed to be listening carefully. _____, researchers found that there was no electrical activity in their brains. (for example / however)

Reading Skill

Distinguishing Facts from Opinions

It's important to distinguish between facts and opinions when you are reading. An **opinion** expresses a person's attitude about something. When people give an opinion, they often use words and phrases like these:

In my opinion	I feel	could
It's my opinion that	might	should
I think	may	ought to

Example: "We **ought to** be learning new languages between ages zero and seven."

A **fact** expresses what can be proven to be true. Writers often use the simple present form of verbs to state facts. This signals that the writer views the statement as a fact or general truth.

Example: "If a child regularly **hears** two languages, her brain **forms** a different pathway for each language."

A. Analyze the Reading

Are these sentences facts or opinions? Underline the words that help you to know.

1. Insights about what is happening in the brains of babies might help kids with learning disabilities.

2. Such studies show that, up to about six months of age, babies can recognize all the sounds that make up all the languages in the world.

3. For teenagers and adults who want to learn new languages, baby studies may offer some useful tips.

4. Researchers have found that it is far better for a language learner to talk with people who speak the language than to rely on educational CDs and DVDs with recorded conversations.

5. When infants watched someone speaking a foreign language on TV, Kuhl found, they had a completely different experience than they did if they watched the same speaker in real life.

B. Apply the Reading Skill

Read the blog and comments and underline the opinions. Then add your opinion to the blog.

| Home | News | Business | Sports | Entertainment | Health | Blog | A&E/Living |

Robots Are Now Teaching English!

Get ready. Robots are about to invade our classrooms. From Korea to Japan to the United States, schools are putting English-speaking robots in front of their students. In Korea, robots are the new teaching assistants in a number of preschools and kindergartens. The young students say that the robots are fun, but are these children really learning anything?

I don't think a computer will ever be able to do what a teacher does. A teacher has to be able to respond to students as individuals. Each student is different, and a teacher has to change his or her teaching style to fit the needs of the student. I seriously doubt that a computer will ever be able to do this.

4 Comments on "Robots Are Now Teaching English!"

Sara says:

In my opinion, schools should spend money training human teachers rather than buying robots. Research shows that children learn more from real speakers than from recorded conversations.

Keiko says:

I don't think you can learn a language without real human interaction.

Hassan says:

Robots might be able to help people learn a language, but I don't think they should replace teachers.

Nancy says:

I think robots might be very helpful in the classroom. A child might be less afraid to make a mistake in front of a robot than in front of a real person.

Add a comment

Discussion & Writing

1. What do you think the future of robots in the classroom is? Do you think they will become more common? Why or why not? Would you like to learn a language from a robot?

2. Think about your experience learning English and take notes in the chart below.

a. When did you start learning English?	
b. What do you remember about your first experience studying English?	
c. What have you found helpful in learning English? What have you found unhelpful?	

3. Write a paragraph describing your experience learning English. Then read your paragraph to a classmate and talk about the similarities and differences in your experiences.

Example

I started learning English when I was 13 years old. I studied English in school, and we had an English class twice a week for an hour. Most of the time we did exercises from a book, and we didn't speak much English in class. When I was 15, I went to a different school, and we had English every day for an hour and we only spoke English in class. We also read easy stories in English, and for me, this was a good way to study a foreign language.

Mini-Dictionary
page 163

Words to Remember		
NOUNS	**VERBS**	**ADJECTIVES**
ability	debate	actual
connection	distinguish	complicated
pattern	focus	
	recognize	
	rely	

The Man in the Moon Has Company

Chapter Focus

CONTENT
What you can see when you look at the moon

READING SKILL
Using context clues

BUILDING VOCABULARY
Learning synonyms

"People only see what they are prepared to see."

— Ralph Waldo Emerson, American writer and philosopher (1802–1883)

Before You Read

A. Connect with the topic. What do you know about the moon? Add four things to the list below.

- *The moon is smaller than the Earth.*

- *The craters on the moon were formed when meteorites hit the surface.*

-

-

-

-

B. Pair work. Compare lists with a partner. How many of your ideas are the same?

C. Preview the reading. Skim the reading on pages 43–45 to complete the Previewing Chart below.

Previewing Chart

1. Title of the reading: _____

2. Names of people and places in the reading. (List 3 more.)

   Earth   _____

   _____   _____

3. Key words. (What words appear several times? List 3 more.)

   sea   _____

   _____   _____

4. Look at the illustration on page 43. Based on this, what do you think the reading is probably about?

   _____

   _____

5. Read the first sentence in each paragraph. Now what do you think the reading is probably about?

   _____

   _____

Reading Passage

The Man in the Moon Has Company

by Alan M. Macrobert
from *The Boston Globe*

1   Have you ever really looked at the moon? Really looked? You might be surprised at how much you can see.

    The moon is the only world beyond the Earth whose landscape is laid out for view with the naked eye.[1] If your eyesight is normal (or well-
5 corrected by glasses), you can make out a great many features on the moon's face—plains, mountainous regions, and the marks of meteorite impacts. The most obvious markings are dark gray patches. These are flat plains of lava,[2] but 17th century astronomers using the newly invented telescope assumed they were water. They named each spot as if it were
10 a sea, *mare* in Latin (pronounced mah-ray).

    The accompanying diagram identifies the largest "seas." *Mare Tranquillitatis*, the Sea of Tranquility, is famous as the site where Neil Armstrong first set foot in 1969. To its upper left is *Mare Serenitatis*, the Sea of Serenity, and *Mare Imbrium*, the Sea of Rains.
15 All three are roughly circular, the result of lava's flooding gigantic craters left by meteorite impacts when the moon was young. To their left is the larger, more formless *Oceanus Procellarum*, the Ocean of Storms, with *Mare Humorum* (Sea of Moisture) and *Mare Numbium* (Sea of Clouds) below it. The large bright areas are mountainous,
20 cratered terrain made of lighter colored rock. Tiny bright patches in *Oceanus Procellarum* are splashes of bright-colored rock kicked up by the formation of individual craters.

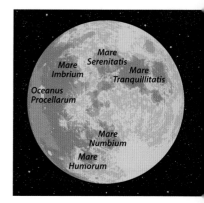

    With a little imagination, the gray seas suggest a face, the familiar man in the moon with his lopsided[3] smile and weepy eyes. We are born with
25 a brain that tries to find meaning everywhere, even in the most random, meaningless patterns—and human faces are what we are programmed to recognize most readily of all. So most people have no trouble seeing the man in the moon, with his enigmatic, clownish grin.[4]

Culture and Language Notes page 145

---

[1] **is laid out for view with the naked eye**   can be seen without any special equipment

[2] **lava**   fluid rock from a volcano

[3] **lopsided**   crooked

[4] **enigmatic, clownish grin**   puzzling smile like a clown's

Other cultures have seen other shapes in this celestial **Rorschach test**.
30   A surprisingly wide variety of peoples saw a rabbit in the moon.
According to the **Aztecs**, the moon was pure white until one of their gods
flung a rabbit against it. In India, the story goes that a rabbit leaped into a
fire to sacrifice himself to feed a starving beggar. The beggar turned out to
be the god **Indra** in disguise. He put the rabbit on the moon so all could
35   remember its act of generosity. In ancient China, the rabbit was carried
there by the moon goddess **Heng O**, who was fleeing her angry husband.
The Chinese also saw a toad in the moon. Others have seen an old man
carrying sticks, a beetle, and a woman reading a book.

The ancient Greeks weren't satisfied with this sort of fantasy. Some
40   wanted to know what the spots actually were. One idea was that they were
reflections of the Earth's continents and seas. But others showed that this
was not possible. Pluto of Chaeronea, a Romanized Greek who lived from
about 46 to 120 CE, wrote a book titled *On the Face of the Disk of the
Moon*. He reported a wide variety of opinions about the moon and gave
45   arguments for and against each. He refuted some of those theories, such
as the one that the markings were illusions in the eye of the beholder.[5]
Instead he suggested, rightly, that the light and dark areas are composed
of different materials. He demonstrated that the moon's phases prove it to
be a solid, opaque[6] sphere with a rough surface lit by sunlight, an object
50   very much like the Earth. Extending this analogy, he declared that the
moon was covered with mountains and valleys. This very correct idea
may have been suggested by the small irregularities that can be seen in the
moon's straight edge near its quarter phases. They are indeed shadows cast
by lunar mountains.

---

[5] **in the eye of the beholder**   in the mind of the person looking
[6] **opaque**   not allowing light to pass through

55 **Plutarch** recorded some even more remarkable ancient findings. He quotes **Aristarchus** as determining the moon to be between 0.31 and 0.40 the size of the Earth (close enough; the true value is 0.27). He cites an unidentified philosopher who measured the moon's distance to be, in modern units, about 215,000 miles (the true value averages 240,000).

60 All this was done with nothing but the naked eye, probably some crude sighting tools, and an excellent knowledge of geometry by people who had outgrown tales about faces and rabbits.

Today we're spoiled by technology. People think they can't see anything in the sky without a telescope, much less figure out what it is. But a good 65 eye and brain can go a long way.

 Word Count: 759 | Reading Time: _____ (Minutes) | Words per Minute: _____ (Word Count/Reading Time)

After You Read
Understanding the Text

A. Comprehension
For each item below, fill in the correct circle.

1. **Finding the Main Idea** Which statement best identifies the main idea of the article?

   Ⓐ It's important to learn about the moon.

   Ⓑ People from different cultures have imagined different things on the face of the moon.

   Ⓒ It is possible to learn a lot about the moon without a telescope.

   Ⓓ The ancient Greeks knew a lot about the moon.

2. **Scanning for Details** According to the article, the telescope was invented ___.

   Ⓐ by the ancient Greeks

   Ⓑ in the first century

   Ⓒ in the 1600s

   Ⓓ in the 18th century

3. **Scanning for Details** Which of these statements is not true about the Sea of Tranquility?

   Ⓐ It is where the first person on the moon landed.

   Ⓑ It is filled with water.

   Ⓒ It was formed when a meteorite hit the moon.

   Ⓓ It is one of the largest "seas" on the moon.

4. **Making Inferences** You can infer from the article that Pluto of Chaeronea ____.

    Ⓐ was a very rich man

    Ⓑ wasn't interested in the opinions of others

    Ⓒ was an independent thinker

    Ⓓ had traveled widely

5. **Identifying the Author's Purpose** The author's purpose in writing this article was most likely to ____.

    Ⓐ explain the importance of telescopes

    Ⓑ convince people that we don't know much about the moon

    Ⓒ show how people from different cultures see different things

    Ⓓ encourage people to really look at the moon

B. Vocabulary: Word Forms

Look back over the reading to find the missing word forms in the chart below.

Noun	Verb	Adjective
1. mountain		
2. assumption		
3. identification		identifiable
4.	imagine	imaginary
5.		generous
6.	fantasize	fantastic
7.	reflect	reflective
8.		irregular
9. remark	remark	
10. excellence	excel	

C. Consider the Issues

Work with a partner to answer the questions below.

1. Look again at the title of the article. Why do you think the author chose this title? How do you think it relates to the information in the article?

2. The author describes the different things that people have seen in the face of the moon. Why do you think he provides this information? What point might he be trying to make?

3. The author says that we are spoiled by technology. What do you think he means? Do you agree or disagree with him? Why?

Building Vocabulary

Learning Synonyms

Synonyms are words that are similar in meaning. For example, the words *assumed*, *thought*, and *believed* are synonyms. They don't mean exactly the same thing, but they are close in meaning.

You can expand your vocabulary by keeping lists of synonyms for common words.

Example

New Word	Synonyms
assumed	thought, believed
flat	smooth
normal	regular, ordinary

A. Look back through the reading on pages 43–45 to find the synonyms below.

1. In paragraph 2, find a synonym for the word *clear*.

_____

2. In paragraph 3, find a synonym for the phrase *very big*.

_____

3. In paragraph 3, find a word that is similar in meaning to *single*.

_____

4. In paragraph 4, find a synonym for the word *easily*.

_____

5. In paragraph 5, find a word that is similar in meaning to *threw*.

_____

6. In paragraph 5, find a synonym for the word *jumped*.

_____

7. In paragraph 6, find a word that is similar in meaning to *correctly*.

_____

8. In paragraph 7, find a synonym for the word *unusual*.

_____

Reading Skill

Using Context Clues

As you learned in Chapter 1, you can use context (the surrounding words and ideas) to guess the meanings of unfamiliar words. These are some common types of context clues that can help you understand new words as you read:

Common Context Clues	Examples
A definition	You can see a lot with the **naked eye**. <u>With normal eyesight</u>, you can make out many features on the face of the moon.
An example	Plutarch recorded some remarkable ancient **findings**, <u>such as the size of the moon and the moon's distance from Earth</u>.
The subject and object of an unfamiliar verb	He suggested that the <u>light and dark areas</u> of the moon **are composed of** <u>different materials</u>.
Contrasting words	They <u>weren't sure</u> what it was, but they **assumed** it was water.
Words in a series	Its **rough**, <u>mountainous</u> surface led people to see different things.
Cause and effect	His **enigmatic** smile <u>confused us</u> completely.

A. Analyze the Reading

Read these sentences from the article and use context to guess the meaning of each boldfaced word. Then look up each word in a dictionary to check your guess.

1. "If your eyesight is normal (or well-corrected by glasses), you can make out a great many **features** on the moon's face—plains, mountainous regions, and the marks of meteorite impacts." (Look for examples.)

   My guess: _____

   Dictionary definition: _____

2. "We are born with a brain that tries to find meaning everywhere, even in the most **random**, meaningless patterns—and human faces are what we are programmed to recognize most readily of all." (Look for words in a series.)

   My guess: _____

   Dictionary definition: _____

3. "In ancient China, the rabbit was carried there by the moon goddess Heng O, who was **fleeing** her angry husband." (Look at the subject and object of a verb.)

My guess: _____

Dictionary definition: _____

4. "The Chinese also saw a toad in the moon. Others have seen an old man carrying sticks, a beetle, and a woman reading a book. The ancient Greeks weren't satisfied with this sort of **fantasy**." (Look for examples.)

My guess: _____

Dictionary definition: _____

5. "He reported a wide variety of opinions about the moon and gave arguments for and against each. He **refuted** some of those theories, such as the one that the markings were illusions in the eye of the beholder. Instead he suggested, rightly, that the light and dark areas are composed of different materials." (Look for contrasting information.)

My guess: _____

Dictionary definition: _____

B. Apply the Reading Skill

Read these sentences about the moon and use context to guess the meaning of each boldfaced word. Underline the words that helped you to guess.

Interesting Facts About the Moon

1. We always see the same side of the Moon; the other side is always **hidden**.

    hidden means _____

2. When Alan Shepard was on the moon, he **drove** a golf ball nearly one half a mile.

    drove means _____

3. The footprints of the Apollo astronauts will not **erode** because there is no wind or water on the moon. The footprints could stay there for 10 million years.

    erode means _____

4. Flying once around the moon is **equivalent** to flying from New York to London and back.

    equivalent means _____

Discussion & Writing

1. What do these quotations mean to you? How does each one relate to the ideas in the reading?

   "There are three classes of people: those who see, those who see when they are shown, those who do not see."
   —Leonardo da Vinci, Italian artist and scientist

   "What you see and hear depends a good deal on where you are standing."
   —C.S. Lewis, British writer

   "We don't see things as they are, we see them as we are."
   —Anaïs Nin, French writer

2. Look at each of the pictures below and describe what you see. (There is no right or wrong answer.) Then compare descriptions with a partner. What do you think your descriptions say about you and your partner?

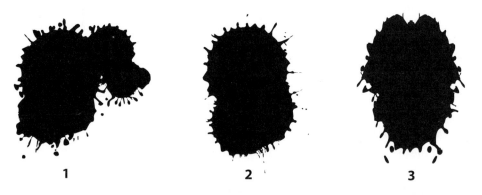

1   2   3

Words to Remember

Mini-Dictionary
page 163

NOUNS	VERBS	ADJECTIVES
argument	assume	bright
diagram	determine	familiar
feature	identify	normal
imagination	program	obvious
landscape	satisfy	remarkable
region	spoil	
theory		

Culture Shock

> **"Culture is everything. Culture is the way we dress, the way we carry our heads, the way we walk, the way we tie our ties."**
> — Aimé Césaire, French writer (1913–2008)

Before You Read

A. **Connect with the topic.** Which of these sentences describe your lifestyle? Check (✓) them. Then compare answers with a partner.

- ☐ I'm always busy.
- ☐ I'm time-oriented. (I'm always checking the time.)
- ☐ I spend a lot of time talking to my friends.
- ☐ I enjoy sitting around and doing nothing.
- ☐ I enjoy eating a good meal.
- ☐ School is an important part of my life.
- ☐ I have a relaxed lifestyle.

B. **Pair work.** "Culture shock" is a popular term used to talk about how people react when they are in a foreign country. What do you think it means? Talk about some possible definitions.

C. **Preview the reading.** Skim the reading on pages 53–55 to complete the Previewing Chart below.

Previewing Chart

1. Title of the reading: _____

2. Names of places in the reading. (List 3 more.)

   Melbourne

   _____

   _____

   _____

3. Key words. (What words appear several times? List 3 more.)

   student

   _____

   _____

   _____

4. Read the first sentence in each paragraph. What do you think the reading is probably about?

_____

_____

_____

Reading Passage

Culture Shock

by Bob Weinstein
from *The Boston Globe*

1   Saying Tamara Blackmore experienced **culture shock** when she arrived here last September is an understatement. It was more like culture trauma[1] for this adventurous student who left **Melbourne's** Monash University to spend her junior year at **Boston College** (BC). Blackmore,

5   20, was joined at BC by 50 other **exchange students** from around the world. Like the thousands of exchange students who enroll in American colleges each year, Blackmore discovered firsthand[2] there is a sea of difference[3] between reading about and experiencing America firsthand. She felt the difference as soon as she stepped off the plane.

10   As soon as she landed in **Boston**, Blackmore could feel the tension in the air. She was about to taste a lifestyle[4] far more hectic than the one she left. "Driving in Boston is crazy," says Blackmore. "It took me a while to get used to the roads and the driving style here. I was always afraid someone was going to hit me. It was

15   particularly tricky since the steering wheel was on the wrong side of the car. In **Australia**, it's on the right side."

      Beyond the cars and traffic jams, Blackmore said it took a while to get used to so many people in one place, all of whom seemed like they were moving at warp speed.[5] "There are only 18 million

20   people in Australia spread out over an entire country," she says, "compared to more than six million people in the state of **Massachusetts** alone. We don't have the kind of congestion you have in Boston. There is a whole different perception of space."

      The pressing problem for Blackmore was making a quick adjustment

25   to the American lifestyle that felt like it was run by a stopwatch. For this easygoing Australian, Americans seemed like perpetual-motion machines.[6] "Americans are very time-oriented," Blackmore says.

🌐 Maps
pages 160–161

Culture and
Language Notes
page 146

---

[1] **culture trauma** extreme form of "culture shock"
[2] **discovered firsthand** learned by directly seeing or experiencing
[3] **sea of difference** very big difference
[4] **taste a lifestyle** experience a way of life
[5] **moving at warp speed** traveling very, very quickly
[6] **perpetual-motion machines** machines that never stop moving

"Everything is done according to a schedule. They're always busy, which made me feel guilty about wanting to just sit around and occasionally
30 watch television. Australians, on the other hand, value their leisure time. The pace there is a lot slower because we don't feel the need to always be busy. It's not that Australians are lazy, it's just that they have a different concept of how time should be spent. Back home, I used to spend a lot more time just talking to my friends."

35 It didn't take long for Blackmore to adjust to American rhythms.[7] "I felt the pressure to work harder and do more because everyone was running around doing so much," she says. When BC students weren't huddled over books, Blackmore found it odd that they were compulsively jogging, running, biking, or doing aerobics in order to be thin. "Compared to
40 home, the girls here are very skinny," she says. "Before I got here, I heard a lot of stories about the pressure to be thin and that many young American women have **eating disorders**. I'll go out with a friend and just tuck into a good meal[8] and have a good time, whereas an American girl would just pick at her food."[9]

45 But it's BC's laid-back[10] and friendly learning environment that sets it apart from her Melbourne college experience. "Generally speaking, learning facilities are a lot better in Boston," she says. "In Australia, students and teachers have little contact outside the classroom. It's a formal and depersonalized relationship. College is a place you go for
50 a few hours every day and then go home. Your social life and school life are separate."

It's just the opposite at BC, according to Blackmore. "BC students and faculty are like one big happy family," she says. "There is a real sense of team spirit. It's like we're all in this together. Going to school here is a
55 lifestyle, whereas at home we're just a number. We attend school to get a degree so we can graduate, get a job, and get on with our lives."[11]

Another pleasant shocker[12] was the close and open relationships American students enjoy with their teachers. It's a sharp contrast to Australia, where college students keep a discreet but respectful distance
60 from their teachers. "I was surprised when I learned students go out to dinner with their lecturers," she says. "We just don't do that back home. Professors deal with hundreds of students, and you're lucky if they remember your name."

---

[7] **adjust to American rhythms** get used to American lifestyles
[8] **tuck into a good meal** enjoy a meal (Australian expression)
[9] **pick at her food** eat only a small amount of food on her plate
[10] **laid-back** relaxed
[11] **get on with our lives** move ahead in our lives
[12] **shocker** surprise

When Blackmore returns to Australia at the end of the school year,
65 she'll have plenty of memories, most of them good ones. BC, like most
American colleges, has gone out of its way to create a memorable
experience for Blackmore and its other exchange students.

 Word Count: 764 | Reading Time: _____ | Words per Minute: _____
(Minutes) | (Word Count/Reading Time)

About the Author

Bob Weinstein is a New York journalist who writes *Tech Watch*, a weekly
syndicated column. He wrote this article for *The Boston Globe*, a major daily
newspaper in Boston, Massachusetts, in the United States.

After You Read
Understanding the Text

A. Comprehension
For each item below, fill in the correct circle.

1. **Scanning for Details** Which of these statements is not true according to
   Tamara Blackmore?
   Ⓐ Boston is very crowded.
   Ⓑ Americans are always in a hurry.
   Ⓒ Americans spend a lot of time talking to friends.
   Ⓓ There are a lot of traffic jams in Boston.

2. **Identifying Pronoun References** The word *they* in line 19 refers to ____.
   Ⓐ cars
   Ⓑ traffic jams
   Ⓒ people
   Ⓓ places

3. **Using Context** The word *congestion* in line 22 is closest in meaning to ____.
   Ⓐ problems
   Ⓑ entertainment
   Ⓒ overcrowding
   Ⓓ relationships

4. **Scanning for Details** According to Blackmore, in Australia ____.
   - Ⓐ students and teachers sometimes become friends
   - Ⓑ professors usually know their students' names
   - Ⓒ universities are better
   - Ⓓ there is a clear separation between academic and social lives

5. **Making Inferences** Blackmore would probably agree that ____.
   - Ⓐ Americans are better drivers than Australians
   - Ⓑ Americans think it's important to keep busy
   - Ⓒ Americans are more laid-back than Australians
   - Ⓓ American women eat more than Australian women

6. **Identifying the Author's Purpose** The purpose of the reading is to ____.
   - Ⓐ demonstrate that Americans study hard and exercise a lot
   - Ⓑ point out some ways in which foreigners experience culture shock in the United States
   - Ⓒ argue that everyone should spend a year as a foreign exchange student
   - Ⓓ compare schools in the United States and Australia

B. Consider the Issues

Work with a partner to answer the questions below.

1. What did you learn about life in the United States and Australia? Complete the chart below with information from the reading on pages 53–55.

Topics	in the United States	in Australia
driving and traffic	There are lots of traffic jams. The steering wheel is on the left side of the cars.	There aren't a lot of traffic jams. The steering wheel is on the right side of the cars.
the pace of life		
free time activities		
university culture		

2. Blackmore noticed many cultural differences between Australia and the United States. Which differences do you think were easy for her to get used to? Which do you think were difficult? Why?

3. From what Blackmore says, do you think that university life in your country is more similar to university life in Australia or the United States? Why?

Building Vocabulary

> **Learning Collocations**
>
> When you are learning a new word, it is helpful to learn the words that are commonly used with it. For example, the verb *have* and the adjective *close* are frequently used with the noun *relationship* as in the sentence below.
>
> - American students often *have* a *close relationship* with their teachers.

A. Scan the reading on pages 53–55 to write the missing adjectives in the spaces below.

1. a ___pressing___ problem (paragraph 4)

2. make a _____ adjustment (paragraph 4)

3. a _____ learning environment (paragraph 6)

4. have _____ contact (paragraph 6)

5. a _____ relationship (paragraph 6)

6. enjoy a _____ relationship with (paragraph 8)

7. a _____ contrast to (paragraph 8)

8. keep a _____ distance from (paragraph 8)

9. a _____ experience (paragraph 9)

B. Complete the questions with an adjective from the chart above. (More than one adjective may be possible.) Then take turns asking and answering the questions with a partner.

1. With whom do you have a _____ relationship?

2. Does your school have a _____ learning environment?

3. Do students in your school have _____ contact with their teachers outside of class?

4. Do you think students should keep a _____ distance from their teachers?

5. What is your most _____ experience of last year?

Reading Skill

Finding the Topic and Main Idea

The *topic* of a piece of writing is its subject—what the writing is about.

The *main idea* of a piece of writing is the writer's message about the topic. The main idea is sometimes, but not always, stated directly in the text. Often you must infer the main idea from several sentences.

When you need to identify the main idea of a paragraph, it often helps to first identify the topic and then ask yourself what the writer's message is.

Example

In the article on pages 53–55, the topic of paragraph 2 is "driving in Boston." The main idea of the paragraph is that "driving in Boston is different from driving in Australia."

A. Analyze the Reading

Look back at the reading on pages 53–55 to complete the chart below.

Paragraph #	Topic	Main Idea
2	driving in Boston	*Driving in Boston is different from driving in Australia.*
3	observations about space	
4	adjusting to the American lifestyle	
5		
6		
7		
8		

B. Apply the Reading Skill

Read each paragraph below and identify the topic and main idea.

As an exchange student in the United States, I spent several months at an American high school. American schools are very different from schools in Turkey. I was surprised to find that students were always asking their teachers questions and expressing their opinions about things. They were very talkative and seemed to enjoy discussing their ideas with each other in class. Additionally, they often got together in groups after class to compare class notes. I was also surprised to find that high school students could choose some of their classes. In Turkey, students may choose a "track," or a program such as math, science, social sciences, or language, but they don't choose their classes. Finally, the students at my American school wore regular clothes. This was a big change for me because students in my country wear school uniforms.

Topic: high schools in Turkey and the United States

Main Idea: _____

For someone from Tokyo, Japan, it takes time to adjust to living in New York City. Even though Tokyo is an expensive city, I was surprised to see how much everything costs in New York. It is difficult for a student to find an inexpensive place to live, and the food in grocery stores is expensive too. A major difference I noticed between Tokyo and New York is the diversity. In New York, you see people from every background and culture, and you hear languages from all over the world. It's impossible to feel like an outsider in New York because everyone is different.

Topic: _____

Main Idea: _____

Discussion & Writing

1. Based on Tamara Blackmore's comments in the reading, would you rather study for a year in Australia or the United States? Why?

2. Have you ever experienced culture shock? Describe your experience. Which country were you in? How long were you there? What are your most positive and negative memories of the experience?

3. Imagine that Tamara Blackmore is coming to your country to study for a year. What information and advice can you give her? What can you tell her about the food, the students, the professors, and other aspects of university life in your country? Write an e-mail message to her with your expert advice.

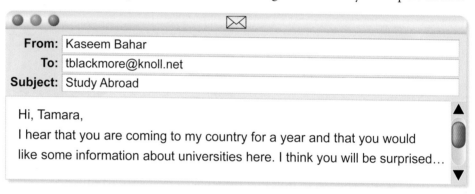

From: Kaseem Bahar
To: tblackmore@knoll.net
Subject: Study Abroad

Hi, Tamara,
I hear that you are coming to my country for a year and that you would like some information about universities here. I think you will be surprised…

4. Think of a country where you would like to study or work for a year. What would you do to prepare for living in this country? Make a list of five questions you have about life in this country and then research the answers to these questions.

Mini-Dictionary
page 163

Words to Remember

NOUNS	VERBS	ADJECTIVES
concept	adjust	entire
contact	deal with	formal
environment	discover	odd
pace	value	
pressure		
relationship		
space		
spirit		
style		
tension		

Private Lives

Chapter Focus

CONTENT
Having a special place to
go to reflect on life

READING SKILL
Identifying supporting ideas

BUILDING VOCABULARY
Learning noun suffixes

"**Solitude is good company.**"
— Luis Barragan, Mexican architect (1902–1988)

Before You Read

A. **Connect with the topic.** Think about one of your favorite places—somewhere you love to go—and answer the questions below.

1. Where is this place?	
2. How often do you go there?	
3. What do you do there?	
4. Why is this one of your favorite places?	

B. **Pair work.** Tell your partner about the place you described in Activity A. Listen to your partner's description of their favorite place and ask three questions to get more information.

C. **Preview the reading.** Skim the reading on pages 63–64 to complete the Previewing Chart below.

Previewing Chart

1. Title of the reading: _____

2. Names of people and places in the reading. (List 5 more.)

    Gulf of Mexico   _____

    _____   _____

    _____   _____

3. Key words. (What words appear several times? List 5 more.)

    parents   _____

    _____   _____

    _____   _____

4. Read the first sentence in each paragraph. What do you think the reading is probably about?

    _____

    _____

    _____

Reading Passage

Private Lives

by Diane Daniel
from the *St. Petersburg Times*

1   *Life seems a little less fragile[1] when you can depend on a special place to always be there for you.*

There is a tiny slice of the **Gulf of Mexico** that belongs to me. Looking across the water, or down the shoreline, I see the past
5   20 years play over and over,[2] like an old **Super 8 movie**.

I'm 16, writing poetry while sitting on a bench at sunset. I'm floating atop the salty sea on my yellow raft. I'm sitting at the water's edge, gathering a rainbow of shells. I'm in college, burgundy hair glistening.[3] I'm a working woman, thinking about my career, paying
10   the bills. I'm heavy, I'm thin. My hair is long, short, long again. I'm happy, sad. Growing older, growing up.

My parents and I moved from **North Carolina** to St. Petersburg, **Florida**, when I was just about to start my senior year of high school. It was a difficult time to be uprooted; I had lived in North Carolina
15   all my life. But I loved the water, so Florida seemed an okay place to live. I can't remember how I first chose my special beach at the end of Eighth Avenue. But once I chose my spot, I never switched beaches.

Almost daily, I swam and sunned there. I watched the sun set. I thought about life. On weekend nights in college, I hung out[4] at the beach with
20   friends, playing music or just listening to the waves. My bedroom at my parents' house holds no memories for me. My memories of Florida are all a mile away, at Eighth Avenue beach.

I live in Boston now and visit my parents in Florida twice a year. Whenever I visit, I spend many hours at my beach, usually under a hot
25   sun, but sometimes at night, when the sand is cool and the sea seems to offer answers it won't share during the day. I go to my beach not only to relax and think, but also to feed off the sea.[5] The waves are gentle, the water soothing. But more important to me is the sea's permanence and sheer force.[6] I want to be strong like that.

 Map page 161

Culture and
Language Notes
page 148

---

[1] **fragile**   easily hurt or broken
[2] **play over and over**   repeat themselves many times
[3] **burgundy hair glistening**   red hair shining
[4] **hung out**   relaxed
[5] **feed off the sea**   get energy and inspiration from the ocean
[6] **sheer force**   great strength

63

30   During one visit to Florida last year, I was sad about the end of a relationship, and I knew that my sadness would worry my parents. I had to stop at Eighth Avenue before I could see them. After flying in from Boston, I drove straight to the beach. It was late afternoon in May, and the sun had softened. When I reached the beach, I parked at the end of Eighth

35 Avenue and slowly walked barefoot to the water. I tasted the Gulf, and with it, some hope.

    I have taken a few friends to my sanctuary,[7] but it's not a place I share with many. Five years ago I brought Jack, a former **boyfriend**, and I'm glad I did. Now when I look down the shore or across the water, he is

40 there, too, laughing at the pelicans as they dive for food, holding me while we watch the sunset from the edge of the water.

    Jack will always be there. So will my friend JoEllen, who came to Eighth Avenue with me a couple of years ago. We walked and walked until the sun and sand had exhausted us. Sometimes I talk my mother into[8] going to

45 watch the sunset, and we sit on the bench, appreciating our time together.

    Last year, I had planned to take Tom to Eighth Avenue. He was going to be the most important visitor of all, the person I thought I would spend the rest of my life with. A few days before we were supposed to leave, he changed his mind, about the trip to Florida and about us. I'm glad he

50 never saw my beach.

    As long as my parents are alive, I will go to Eighth Avenue. It has occurred to me that I will probably mourn their deaths there, listening to the waves and watching the gulls. I wonder how often I will see my beach after my parents are gone. I'm sure I will go there from time to time, maybe

55 even stay in one of the cottages nearby that I've passed so often. But it doesn't matter. My tiny slice of the Gulf of Mexico is always within reach.

Word Count: 706   Reading Time: _____   Words per Minute: _____
                               (Minutes)   (Word Count/Reading Time)

About the Author

Diane Daniel (1957–) is a freelance writer. She was married near Eighth Avenue at Indian Rocks Beach in 2004, a decade after this essay was written.

---

7 **sanctuary**   safe, protected place
8 **talk my mother into**   convince my mother to

After You Read

Understanding the Text

A. Comprehension

For each item below, fill in the correct circle.

1. **Finding the Main Idea** The main idea of this reading is:
   - Ⓐ You should only bring a few close friends to your special place.
   - Ⓑ The Eighth Avenue beach has played an important role in the author's life for the past 20 years.
   - Ⓒ You need to be alone to solve your problems.
   - Ⓓ When you end a significant relationship, it's a good idea to spend time alone at your special place.

2. **Scanning for Details** The author chose her special beach when she ___, and she never changed beaches after that.
   - Ⓐ started high school
   - Ⓑ moved to North Carolina
   - Ⓒ was in college
   - Ⓓ moved to Florida

3. **Scanning for Details** The author has already done all of the following at the Eighth Avenue beach except:
   - Ⓐ play music and write poetry
   - Ⓑ watch the sunset with a boyfriend
   - Ⓒ mourn the death of a family member
   - Ⓓ take long walks and collect shells

4. **Making Inferences** In line 42, the sentence, "Jack will always be there," means:
   - Ⓐ Jack lives near the Eighth Avenue beach.
   - Ⓑ Jack accompanies the author to her special beach every time she goes.
   - Ⓒ When the author visits her beach, she remembers the time she spent there with Jack.
   - Ⓓ Visiting the Eighth Avenue beach was the highlight of the author's relationship with Jack.

5. **Making Inferences** All of the following statements are probably true about the author except:
   - Ⓐ She has positive feelings about Jack.
   - Ⓑ She has always liked the ocean.
   - Ⓒ She and Tom had talked about getting married.
   - Ⓓ She has always been slim.

6. Understanding Tone The overall tone of this reading is:

ⓐ personal and narrative

ⓑ serious and informative

ⓒ sad and depressing

ⓓ light and romantic

B. Vocabulary: Using Context

In the sentences below, use context to guess the general meanings of the italicized words. Then underline the word(s) that helped you to guess the meanings.

1. I'm floating atop the salty sea on my yellow *raft*.

ⓐ a bathing suit

ⓑ a type of fish

ⓒ a type of boat

2. I go to the beach not only to relax and think, but also to feed off the sea. The waves are gentle, the water *soothing*.

ⓐ calming

ⓑ dangerous

ⓒ frightening

3. Now when I look down the shore or across the water, Jack is there, too, laughing at the *pelicans* as they dive for food.

ⓐ a type of bird

ⓑ a type of boat

ⓒ a type of tree

4. As long as my parents are alive, I will go to Eighth Avenue. It has occurred to me that I will probably *mourn* their deaths there, listening to the waves and watching the gulls.

ⓐ feel sad about

ⓑ feel happy about

ⓒ stop thinking about

C. Consider the Issues

Work with a partner to answer the questions below.

1. Why does the author keep going back to the beach?

2. What qualities of the sea are important for the author? Why?

3. Why do you think the author is glad that Tom never saw her beach?

Building Vocabulary

A. Write the noun forms of the words below. Then think of another noun for each suffix.

Verb + *-ence* = Noun	Verb + *-ment* = Noun	Verb + *-ation* = Noun
occur _occurrence_	pay _____	relax _____
difference	_____	_____

Verb + *-tion* / *-ion* = Noun	Adjective + *ness* = Noun	Adjective + *-ance* = Noun
exhaust _____	sad _____	important _____
appreciate _____	gentle _____	_____
_____	_____	

B. Use the noun form of the boldfaced verb or adjective in the first sentence to complete the second sentence.

1. If you **appreciate** the things your parents do for you, you should show it.

   You should show _____ for the things your parents do for you.

2. You should avoid getting **exhausted** in hot weather. It can be dangerous.

   Heat _____ can be dangerous and should be avoided.

3. Heavy storms **occur** frequently here in the summer.

   Heavy storms are a common _____ here in the summer.

4. You can **pay** your bill online.

   _____ of your bill can be made online.

5. If you think you don't need time to **relax**, you are wrong.

   It's important to have time for _____.

Reading Skill

> **Identifying Supporting Ideas**
> Writers usually focus on one or two main ideas in a piece of writing. They then support their main ideas with examples and details. These supporting ideas help the reader understand and appreciate the writer's main ideas.

A. Analyze the Reading

Look back at the reading on pages 63–64 and find two more details that support the main idea given below.

Main Idea
The Eighth Avenue beach has played an important role in the author's life for the past 20 years.

Supporting Ideas
1. The author took special people in her life to the beach.
2.
3.

B. Analyze the Reading

Look back at the reading in Chapter 3, "Student Learning Teams" (pages 23–25), and find at least three details that support the main idea given below.

Main Idea
Forming a learning team can improve your academic performance.

Supporting Ideas
1.
2.
3.

C. Apply the Reading Skill

Read the paragraph below and complete the chart. Write the main idea of the paragraph and three supporting ideas.

    Korea is surrounded by ocean on three sides, so it has plenty of wonderful beaches. The best beach, however, is Jungmun Beach on Jeju Island. One thing that distinguishes this beach is the surfing. There are some good waves here, especially between August and October. The strong current along this beach makes it a great place for those who enjoy windsurfing. Another special thing about this beach is its unique sand; it is a mixture of colors—black, white, and red. Jungmun Beach also has many subtropical trees and plants right next to the beach. When you're there, you really feel that you are in an exotic spot. If you get tired of the water, there are also some interesting sights to visit very close to the beach. You can easily get to a nearby waterfall, a small cave, and a hidden cove. If this isn't enough to convince you that Jungmun Beach is the best beach in Korea, consider that Korea's largest triathlon starts here every summer and that many movies and commercials have been filmed at this scenic spot.

Main Idea

Supporting Ideas
1.
2.
3.

Discussion & Writing

1. Complete the chart below with more information about the beach in the reading on pages 63–64. Next, think of a place that is special to you. Add information about this place to the chart below.

Place	Things you can do there	Things you can see	Things you can hear and smell
the Eighth Avenue beach	write poetry swim sunbathe	water	the sound of waves

2. Use the information in the chart above to write a paragraph describing your special place for your classmates and teacher to read. Explain how and why this place is special to you.

Example

There is a beautiful art museum on the south side of my city. It is unlike any other art museum I know because it was once a very wealthy person's house. In the center of the house there is a large garden full of unusual flowers. It's very quiet there; the only thing you hear is the sound of birds. But when you get tired of the garden, you can climb the stairs to one of the large rooms filled with works of art. On a day when I feel stressed or upset, this museum is a perfect place to relax and be inspired by beautiful things.

Mini-Dictionary
page 163

Words to Remember

NOUNS	VERBS	ADJECTIVES
edge	appreciate	gentle
force	depend on	
memory	float	
sadness	gather	
	occur	
	reach	
	switch	

A Young Blind Whiz

Chapter Focus

CONTENT
Talents and abilities

READING SKILL
Identifying pronoun
references

BUILDING VOCABULARY
Understanding compound
nouns

"The same person cannot be skilled
in everything; each has his special
excellence."
— Euripides, Greek playwright (c. 485–406 BCE)

Before You Read

A. Connect with the topic. The reading on pages 73–74 is about a "computer whiz"—someone who is very good with computers. What does it take to be good with computers? Check (✓) the ideas below. Then add two more ideas to the list.

☐ patience ☐ good verbal skills

☐ a good memory ☐ good social skills

☐ creativity ☐ intelligence

☐ interest in technical subjects ☐ a sense of humor

☐ _____ ☐ _____

B. Pair work. Choose the three ideas from Activity A that you and your partner think are the most important characteristics of a computer whiz.

C. Preview the reading. Move your eyes quickly over the reading on pages 73–74 to complete the Previewing Chart below.

Previewing Chart

1. Title of the reading: _____

2. Names of people and places in the reading. (List 3 more.)

    Suleyman Gokyigit

    _____

    _____

    _____

3. Key words. (What words appear several times? List 3 more.)

    computer

    _____

    _____

    _____

4. Read the first paragraph. What would you like to find out about Mr. Gokyigit? (Write 3 more questions.)

    How does he use a computer?

    _____ ?

    _____ ?

    _____ ?

A Young Blind Whiz on Computers

by Tom Petzinger
from *The Wall Street Journal*

1   Sometimes, a perceived disability[1] turns out to be an asset on the job. Though he is only 18 years old and blind, Suleyman Gokyigit (pronounced gok-yi-it) is among the top computer technicians and programmers at InteliData Technologies Corp., a large software company
5 with several offices across the United States.

    "After a merger[2] last October, two disparate computer networks[3] were driving us crazy," recalls Douglas Braun, an InteliData vice president. "We couldn't even send e-mail to each other." In three weeks, Mr. Gokyigit, a University of Toledo **sophomore** who **works part-time**
10 at InteliData's office in the city, created the software needed to integrate the two networks. "None of the company's 350 other employees could have done the job in three months," says Mr. Braun. "Suleyman can literally 'see' into the heart of the computer."

    Mr. Gokyigit's gift, as Mr. Braun calls it, is an unusual ability to
15 conceptualize[4] the innards of[5] a machine. "The computer permits me to reach out into the world and do almost anything I want to do," says Mr. Gokyigit, who is a computer science engineering major with **straight As**.

    Like most blind people who work with computers, Mr. Gokyigit uses a voice-synthesizer that reads the video display on his monitor in a
20 mechanical voice. Devices that produce **Braille** screen displays are also available, but Mr. Gokyigit says they "waste time." Instead, he depends on memory. Turning the synthesizer to top speed, he remembers almost everything he hears, at least until a project is completed. While the synthesizer talks, Mr. Gokyigit mentally "maps" the computer screen
25 with numbered coordinates (such as three across, two down) and memorizes the location of each icon on the grid[6] so he can call up files with his mouse.

🌐 Maps
pages 159, 161

Culture and
Language Notes
page 149

---

[1] **a perceived disability**   something you think of as a negative thing

[2] **merger**   a combining of two or more companies into one

[3] **two disparate computer networks**   two groups of computers that can't communicate with each other

[4] **conceptualize**   form an idea of

[5] **the innards of**   the inside of

[6] **grid**   a pattern of evenly spaced vertical and horizontal lines

The young programmer is also at home with hardware, thanks partly to a highly developed sense of touch. Mitzi Nowakowski, an office manager
30 at InteliData, recalls how he easily disconnected and reconnected their computer systems during a move last year. "Through feel, Suleyman can locate connectors, pins, and wires much faster than most other people with sight," she says.

Mr. Gokyigit was born in **Turkey**, where at age two he developed
35 an eye condition that left him blind. His parents brought him to the Mayo Clinic in the U.S., but nothing could be done. "His doctors kept emphasizing, 'Never shelter him or pity him,'" recalls his father, Hasan. Today, Mr. Gokyigit's co-workers call him "Suleyman the Magnificent," after the 16th century Turkish sultan who greatly expanded the
40 **Ottoman Empire**.

Several months ago, on a trip to San Francisco, Mr. Braun had difficulty accessing the company's mainframe using his laptop. He needed specific numbers to get into four InteliData files. Instead of asking someone to manually search a thick logbook[7] of computer addresses, he called Mr.
45 Gokyigit, who had committed the logbook to memory and produced the proper numbers "in ten seconds," Mr. Braun says.

Much of the student programmer's speed comes from his ability to block out[8] distractions while at the computer. When typing, he listens intently to the synthesizer. His long, thin fingers fly over the keyboard.
50 "Nothing seems to shake his concentration," says Ms. Nowakowski, his immediate boss.[9]

Mr. Gokyigit is the only company employee on call[10] 24 hours a day. "We consider him our top troubleshooter,"[11] says Mr. Braun.

 Word Count: 549 | Reading Time: _____ (Minutes) | Words per Minute: _____ (Word Count/Reading Time)

About the Author

Tom Petzinger has worked for *The Wall Street Journal* as a columnist, editor, and reporter for over 20 years. *The Wall Street Journal* is a leading business publication in the United States. It includes stock quotes, national and international business news and trends, and features articles such as this one on interesting people in the world of business.

---

7 **logbook**   written record of information
8 **block out**   ignore
9 **his immediate boss**   the person he reports directly to
10 **on call**   available to go to work
11 **troubleshooter**   problem solver

After You Read
Understanding the Text

A. Comprehension
For each item below, fill in the correct circle.

1. **Finding the Main Idea** The main idea of this reading is:
   - Ⓐ Suleyman Gokyigit is a very talented computer programmer.
   - Ⓑ Mr. Gokyigit has the unusual ability to visualize the insides of a computer.
   - Ⓒ People have different strengths and abilities.
   - Ⓓ Something you think is a disability might actually be helpful in your job.

2. **Scanning for Details** According to paragraph 4, which of the following statements is true about Mr. Gokyigit?
   - Ⓐ He doesn't use a voice-synthesizer because he thinks it's a waste of time.
   - Ⓑ He uses a Braille screen device to find information on the computer screen.
   - Ⓒ He uses a voice synthesizer that reads aloud the information on the screen.
   - Ⓓ He uses his memory instead of a voice-synthesizer.

3. **Scanning for Details** The author's description of Mr. Gokyigit does not mention which of the following?
   - Ⓐ He was not born in the United States.
   - Ⓑ He earns $25,000 annually.
   - Ⓒ He is a student at the University of Toledo.
   - Ⓓ He is on call 24 hours a day.

4. **Making Inferences** In line 17, the article mentions that Suleyman Gokyigit is a straight-A student in computer science engineering. What can you infer from this?
   - Ⓐ He has a talent for computers.
   - Ⓑ He has a lot of money.
   - Ⓒ He has always gotten good grades.
   - Ⓓ He doesn't need to study very much.

5. **Making Inferences** In line 45, the article mentions that Mr. Gokyigit learned all of the computer addresses in the company's thick logbook. What can you infer from this?
   - Ⓐ He wrote the logbook.
   - Ⓑ It's easy for anyone to learn the logbook.
   - Ⓒ He has a good memory.
   - Ⓓ He learned the computer addresses quickly.

B. Vocabulary: Using Context

Use context clues to guess the meanings of the words below.

1. The word *integrate* in line 10 is closest in meaning to ___.
   - (A) separate
   - (B) bring together
   - (C) make interesting
   - (D) interpret

2. The word *voice-synthesizer* in line 19 describes ___.
   - (A) a mechanical reader
   - (B) a type of Braille
   - (C) a computer monitor
   - (D) a video display

3. The phrase *at home with* in line 28 is similar in meaning to ___.
   - (A) not working with
   - (B) nervous about
   - (C) unfamiliar with
   - (D) comfortable with

4. In line 42, the word *accessing* is closest in meaning to ___.
   - (A) fixing
   - (B) getting into
   - (C) learning about
   - (D) understanding

C. Consider the Issues

Work with a partner to answer the questions below.

1. What are Suleyman Gokyigit's talents and abilities?

2. What can he do better than those with sight?

3. In addition to computer programming, what jobs do you think he would be good at? Why?

4. Choose three adjectives to describe Suleyman Gokyigit. Then tell the class why you chose each word.

Adjectives	Reasons
1.	1.
2.	2.
3.	3.

Building Vocabulary

> ## Understanding Compound Nouns
> Compound nouns are two or more words that function together as one word or concept. Most compound nouns are made up of a *noun + noun* or an *adjective + noun*.
>
> **Examples:** *computer technician*   *video display*   *software*
>
> The first word in a compound noun usually identifies a specific type of the second noun. For example, in the compound noun "computer technician," the word *computer* identifies the type of *technician*. In the compound noun "video display," the word *video* identifies the type of *display*.
>
> Most compound nouns are written either as two separate words (*computer whiz*) or as a single word (*hardware*). A few compound nouns have a hyphen (*voice-synthesizer*).

A. Find a compound noun in the article on pages 73–74 to complete each sentence below.

1. Because Suleyman is so skilled at locating problems and solving them, he is respected as the company's top _____.

2. Suleyman's major at the University of Toledo is _____ _____ engineering.

3. Suleyman is considered among the best _____ _____ and programmers at his company.

4. Although Braille _____ _____ are available, Suleyman prefers to use a voice-synthesizer.

B. Create a compound noun using two nouns from the box below to complete each sentence. The compound noun might be one word, two words, or hyphenated.

office	synthesizer	programmers	computer	voice	lap
work	book	top	manager	net	log

1. Many computers connected to each other are called a computer _____.

2. A _____–_____ reads a video display in a mechanical voice.

3. New software is created each day by _____ _____.

4. A _____ is a thin portable computer.

5. Companies often keep computer addresses in a _____.

6. An _____ _____ is responsible for the office building and supplies.

Reading Skill

Identifying Pronoun References

In writing, it would be very repetitive to use the same noun phrase over and over again, as in Example 1 below. For this reason, writers often replace a noun or noun phrase with a pronoun, as in Example 2. When you are reading, it is important to know who or what each pronoun refers to.

Example 1: Devices that produce Braille screen displays are also available, but Mr. Gokyigit says **devices that produce Braille screen displays** waste time. Instead, **Mr. Gokyigit** depends on memory.

Example 2: Devices that produce Braille screen displays are also available, but Mr. Gokyigit says **they** waste time. Instead, **he** depends on memory.

A. Analyze the Reading

In the sentences from the reading below, identify the word or words that the boldfaced pronouns are referencing.

1. Sometimes, a perceived disability turns out to be an asset on the job. Though **he** is only 18 years old and blind, Suleyman Gokyigit is among the top computer technicians and programmers at InteliData Technologies Corp.

   he refers to _____

2. Mr. Gokyigit's gift, as Mr. Braun calls **it**, is an unusual ability to conceptualize the innards of a machine.

   it refers to _____

3. Mr. Gokyigit was born in Turkey, where at age two **he** developed an eye condition that left **him** blind.

   he and *him* refer to _____

4. Several months ago, on a trip to San Francisco, Mr. Braun had difficulty accessing the company's mainframe using his laptop. **He** needed specific numbers to get into four InteliData files.

   he refers to _____

B. Apply the Reading Skill

What do the boldfaced pronouns in the article below refer to? Write your answers below.

A Two-Year-Old Geography Whiz

Lilly Gaskin is only 26 months old and she is not old enough to really talk, but **she** has already mastered world geography. She can point out almost any country on a map, and she started doing **this** at 16 months.

According to her father James, Lilly's amazing map reading ability came about by accident. "Lilly's uncle went to Thailand when she was 16 months old," **he** explains. "And she wanted to know where **he** went. So we found a map and pointed to Thailand. The next time she saw a map, she pointed **it** out.

"We'll point to a place she doesn't know," says James, "and then we'll ask her where it is, and she'll point to **it**. Then we'll ask her a couple more that she does know. Then we'll go back to the one she didn't know and she's got **it**—takes 20 seconds!" And the rest is history! (Well, geography, really!)

1. she = _____

2. this = _____

3. he = _____

4. he = _____

5. it = _____

6. it = _____

7. it = _____

Discussion & Writing

1. What do these quotations mean to you? How does each one relate to the ideas in the reading?

"If you cannot accomplish a thing, leave it and pass to another which you can accomplish."
—Al Kali, Arab philosopher (901–967)

"It is not enough to have a good mind. The main thing is to use it well."
—René Descartes, French philospher (1596–1650)

"If I have made any valuable discoveries, it has been owing more to patient attention than to any other talent."
—Isaac Newton, English physicist (1642–1727)

2. What are your partner's talents and abilities? Add one or two questions to the chart below. Then interview your partner and check (✓) your partner's answers.

Are you...	Yes	No	Do you have...	Yes	No
good with numbers?			a good memory?		
good at fixing things?			good balance?		
a good typist?			a good voice?		
a good public speaker?			a good imagination?		
well organized?			good concentration?		

Based on your partner's answers, in what profession do you think your partner could best use his or her talents?

Mini-Dictionary
page 163

Words to Remember

NOUNS	VERBS	ADJECTIVES
concentration	emphasize	available
condition	permit	top
device	recall	
location	shelter	
monitor	waste	
network		
system		

How to Make a Speech

Chapter Focus

CONTENT
Preparing and making
a good speech

READING SKILL
Understanding text
organization: Headings

BUILDING VOCABULARY
Understanding multi-word
verbs

"Speech is power: speech is to persuade,
to convert, to compel."

— Ralph Waldo Emerson, American writer and
philosopher (1802–1883)

Before You Read

A. Connect with the topic. Think of a speech you have heard. What was the topic? Who was the audience? Do you think the speech was good, bad, or okay? Why?

B. Pair work. What are the three most important characteristics of a good speech? Check ideas from the list below. Then add your own idea to the list.

☐ Has an interesting topic

☐ Makes the audience feel emotion, such as happiness or fear

☐ Has a clear and logical structure

☐ Teaches people something new

☐ Isn't too long

☐ _____ (Your idea)

Why do you think your three choices are important? Explain your ideas to another pair.

Example
We think it's very important for a speech to have an interesting topic. If the topic isn't good, the speech will be boring.

C. Preview the reading. Skim the reading on pages 83–85 to complete the Previewing Chart below.

Previewing Chart

1. Title of the reading: _____

2. Headings (section titles) in the reading. (List 2 more.)

Why know how to speak?

_____

_____

3. Key words. (What words appear several times? List 5 more.)

topic _____

_____ _____

_____ _____

4. I think this reading is probably about

_____

_____.

Reading Passage

How To Make A Speech
by George Plimpton
from *How to Use the Power of the Printed Word*

1   One of life's terrors for the uninitiated[1] is to be asked to make a speech.

"Why me?" will probably be your first reaction. "I don't have anything to say." The fact is that each one of us has a store of material which should be of interest to others. There is no reason why it should not be adapted to
5   a speech.

Why Know How to Speak?
Scary as it is, it's important for anyone to be able to speak in front of others, whether 20 around a conference table or a hall filled with a thousand faces.

10   Being able to speak can mean better grades in any class. It can mean talking the town council out of[2] increasing your property taxes. It can mean talking top management into[3] buying your plan.

How to Pick a Topic
You were probably asked to speak in the first place in the hope that
15   you would be able to articulate a topic[4] that you know something about. Still, it helps to find out about your audience first. Who are they? Why are they there? What are they interested in? How much do you already know about your subject?

How to Plan What to Say
20   Here is where you must do your homework.

The more you sweat in advance, the less you'll have to sweat once you appear on stage. Research your topic thoroughly. Check the library for facts, quotes, books, and timely magazine and newspaper articles on your subject. Get in touch with experts. Write to them, make phone calls, get
25   interviews to help round out your material. In short, gather—and learn— far more than you'll ever use. You can't imagine how much confidence that knowledge will inspire.

Culture and
Language Notes
page 151

---

1   **the uninitiated**   people doing something for the first time
2   **talking the town council out of**   convincing government officials that something is a bad idea
3   **talking top management into**   convincing your bosses that something is a good idea
4   **articulate a topic**   talk about a subject

Now start organizing and writing. Most authorities suggest that a good speech breaks down into three basic parts: an introduction, the body of the speech, and the summation.

- *Introduction*: An audience makes up its mind very quickly. Once the mood of an audience is set, it is difficult to change it, which is why introductions are important. If the speech is to be lighthearted in tone,[5] the speaker can start off by telling a good-natured story[6] about the subject or himself.

- *Main body*: There are four main intents[7] in the body of the well-made speech. These are (1) to entertain, which is probably the hardest; (2) to instruct, which is the easiest if the speaker has done the research and knows the subject; (3) to persuade, which one does at a sales presentation, a **political rally**, or a town meeting; and finally, (4) to inspire, which is what the speaker emphasizes at a sales meeting, in a **sermon**, or at a **pep rally**.

- *Summation*: An ending should probably incorporate a sentence or two which sounds like an ending—a short summary of the main points of the speech, perhaps, or the repeat of a phrase that most embodies what the speaker has hoped to convey. It is valuable to think of the last sentence or two as something which might produce applause. Phrases which are perfectly appropriate to signal this are: "In closing…" or "I have one last thing to say…"

How to Sound Spontaneous

The best speakers are those who make their words sound spontaneous[8] even if memorized. I've found it's best to learn a speech point by point, not word for word. Careful preparation and a great deal of practicing are required to make it come together smoothly and easily. **Mark Twain** once said, "It takes three weeks to prepare a good ad-lib speech."[9]

Brevity Is an Asset[10]

A sensible plan, if you have been asked to speak to an exact limit, is to talk your speech into a mirror and stop at your allotted time; then cut the speech accordingly. The more familiar you become with your speech, the more confidently you can deliver it.

As anyone who listens to speeches knows, brevity is an asset. Twenty minutes are ideal. An hour is the limit an audience can listen comfortably.

---

[5] **lighthearted in tone**   amusing; not serious

[6] **good-natured story**   funny story

[7] **intents**   purposes

[8] **make their words sound spontaneous**   speak very naturally, like they're having a conversation

[9] **ad-lib speech**   public talk that is not prepared in advance

[10] **brevity is an asset**   shortness is a good thing

How Questions Help

A question period at the end of a speech is a good notion. One would not ask questions following a **tribute to the company treasurer on his retirement**, say, but a technical talk or an informative speech can be enlivened with a question period.

The Crowd

The larger the crowd, the easier it is to speak, because the response is multiplied and increased. Most people do not believe this. They peek out[11] from behind the curtain, and if the audience is filled to the rafters,[12] they begin to moan softly in the back of their throats.

What About Stage Fright?

Very few speakers escape the so-called "butterflies."[13] There does not seem to be any cure for them, except to realize that they are beneficial rather than harmful, and never fatal. The tension usually means that the speaker, being keyed up,[14] will do a better job. **Edward R. Murrow** called stage fright "the sweat of perfection." Mark Twain once comforted a fright-frozen[15] friend about to speak: "Just remember they don't expect much." My own feeling is that with thought, preparation, and faith in your ideas, you can go out there and expect a pleasant surprise.

Word Count: 869 | Reading Time: _____ (Minutes) | Words per Minute: _____ (Word Count/Reading Time)

About the Author

George Plimpton (1927–2003) was a writer, public speaker, editor, and actor who lived in New York. He is best known for participating in many of the activities he wrote about. He trained with a professional football team, boxed three rounds with a light-heavyweight champion, and played on the professional golf circuit.

---

[11] **peek out** look out timidly
[12] **filled to the rafters** full of people
[13] **the so-called "butterflies"** nervous feelings in one's stomach
[14] **keyed up** excited and nervous
[15] **fright-frozen** very nervous or scared

After You Read

Understanding the Text

A. Comprehension
For each item below, fill in the correct circle.

1. **Finding the Main Idea** The main idea of the reading is:
   - (A) It's very difficult to give a good speech.
   - (B) With a lot of research and practice, anyone can learn how to give a good speech.
   - (C) The three basic parts of a speech are the introduction, the main body, and the summation.
   - (D) Choosing a good topic is the most important part of making a good speech.

2. **Scanning for Details** According to the author, the following is the most difficult to accomplish when giving a speech:
   - (A) instruct
   - (B) inspire
   - (C) entertain
   - (D) persuade

3. **Making Inferences** The author would probably agree that:
   - (A) Some people can never be good speakers.
   - (B) Some people are natural speakers and don't need practice.
   - (C) New speakers should first speak to a small audience, and then to a large one.
   - (D) A good introduction is more important than a good summation.

4 **Using Context** The word *persuade* in line 39 is closest in meaning to:
   - (A) excite
   - (B) breathe
   - (C) listen to
   - (D) convince

5. **Understanding Tone** The overall tone of this reading is:
   - (A) serious and academic
   - (B) light and silly
   - (C) informative and humorous
   - (D) scientific and technical

B. Consider the Issues
Work with a partner to answer the questions below.

1. What are the best ways to research a topic before writing a speech?

2. Most people get nervous before giving a speech. What can a speaker do to feel more relaxed and confident?

3. What are some things a person can do to sound spontaneous? Why is it important to sound spontaneous when giving a speech?

Building Vocabulary

Understanding Multi-Word Verbs

Multi-word verbs are made up of a verb and one or more other words. These verbs have a special meaning which is different from the meaning of the individual words. For example, in the sentence below, the verb *talk out of* means *convince not to*.

> Being able to speak well can mean **talking** the town council **out of** increasing your property taxes.

A *phrasal verb* is one type of multi-word verb. A phrasal verb is formed with a verb + adverbial (e.g., *fill in, turn on, bring up, work out*).

A *phrasal-prepositional verb* is another type of multi-word verb. It is formed with a verb + adverbial + preposition (e.g., *get out of, look forward to, come up with*).

A. Scan the reading on pages 83–85 to find the missing word or words in each verb below. Then match each verb to a definition on the right.

Phrasal Verbs and Phrasal-Prepositional Verbs	Meaning
1. talk ___out___ ___of___ _b_ (paragraph 4)	**a.** complete
2. talk _____ ___ (paragraph 4)	**b.** convince not to
3. find _____ ___ (paragraph 5)	**c.** separate into
4. round _____ ___ (paragraph 7)	**d.** learn
5. break _____ _____ ___ (paragraph 8)	**e.** convince
6. start _____ ___ (paragraph 9)	**f.** begin

B. Now use the correct form of a verb from the chart to complete each question below. (More than one verb may be possible.) Then ask a partner the questions.

1. How would you _____ a friend _____ _____ doing something dangerous?

2. How can you _____ _____ where someone lives?

3. How would you like to _____ _____ your education?

4. What is the best way to _____ _____ a vacation?

Reading Skill

Understanding text organization: Headings
You can use headings to help you understand text organization—the structure of a reading passage. A heading is a small group of words that serves as a title for a paragraph or several paragraphs. Headings help you skim a reading to understand "the big picture," or scan it to find specific information.

Example:

Heading ┄┄•
How to Pick a Topic
You were probably asked to speak in the first place in the hope that you would be able to articulate a topic that you know something about. Still, it helps to find out about your audience first. Who are they? Why are they there? What are they interested in? How much do you already know about your subject?

Heading ┄┄•
How to Plan What to Say
Here is where you must do your homework.

A. Analyze the Reading

Scan the reading on pages 83–85 to answer the questions below.

1. How many headings does the author use?

_____

2. Under which heading does the author talk about doing research?

_____

3. Under which heading can you find information on the ideal length for a speech?

_____

4. Why do you think the author chose to use so many headings for this article?

_____

5. Do you think the headings helped you read this article more quickly and effectively? Why or why not?

_____

B. Apply the Reading Skill

Read the first part of the reading below. Then use the six headings in the reading to answer the questions that follow.

SPEAK FOR YOURSELF

Register for a speech contest!
Feeling strongly about an important global issue? Register to compete in the Speak for Yourself speech contest. This contest provides passionate Singaporean youths with a platform to express their views on global and social issues.

But what do I talk about?
You can talk about any global or social issues you are concerned with, such as free trade, globalization, animal rights, online music piracy, youths at risk, just to name a few. After you've identified your issue of concern, you can go on to talk about how you'd go about solving the problem, or why people should be concerned about the issue.

Application process

Rules and regulations

How to submit your audio recording

Prizes

About the Speak for Yourself organization

1. Under which heading can you find information on appropriate topics to speak about?

   But what do I talk about?

2. Which section contains information about the foundation that supports this speech contest?

   _____

3. Where can you learn if there is a registration fee?

   _____

4. Which section tells you if the organization wants you to e-mail a digital recording of your speech?

   _____

5. Where can you find out the minimum and maximum ages of people entering this speech contest?

   _____

Discussion & Writing

1. Prepare a short speech to your classmates. Choose one of the topics below and put a check (✓) beside it. If you have your own idea, write it down.

☐ how to form a study group

☐ how to increase your English vocabulary

☐ how to _____ (your own idea)

2. Write your speech. Like good pieces of writing, most speeches include an introduction, a main body with key points, and a conclusion (summation). Use this model to help you.

Introduction — • Good afternoon! My name is Monica Jones, and I am running for treasurer[16] of our class here at Sweetwater University. I hope you will consider voting for me.

Main Body — • There are three reasons why I would be an excellent treasurer. First, I'm good at math, and I like numbers. I will manage our class's money very carefully.
Second, ...
Third, ...

Conclusion — • In conclusion, I would like to summarize...

3. Stand in front of a mirror and practice your speech. You can also practice with a classmate. Try to learn your speech "point by point, not word for word."

Mini-Dictionary
page 163

Words to Remember		
NOUNS	**VERBS**	**ADJECTIVES**
audience	adapt	appropriate
authority	entertain	exact
cure	organize	ideal
expert	persuade	sensible
knowledge	produce	valuable
limit	signal	
mood		
reaction		

---

16 **treasurer** the person responsible for managing money and payments

Conversational Ball Games

> "If you're going to play the game properly, you'd better know every rule."
> — Barbara Jordan, American politician (1936–1996)

Before You Read

A. **Connect with the topic.** Which statements describe the game of tennis? Which describe bowling? Write *T* (tennis) or *B* (bowling).

_____ **a.** To play, you need a ball and ten pins.

_____ **b.** For this game, you need a ball, a racquet, and a net.

_____ **c.** Players hit the ball back and forth to each other.

_____ **d.** If you miss the ball, your opponent gets a point.

B. **Pair work.** What else do you know about tennis and bowling? Share information with a partner.

C. **Preview the reading.** Look quickly over the reading on pages 93–95 to complete the Previewing Chart below.

Previewing Chart

1. Title of the reading: _____

2. Names of people and places in the reading. (List 2 more.)

   Japan

   _____

   _____

3. Key words. (What words appear several times? List 3 more.)

   ball

   _____

   _____

   _____

4. Read the first paragraph. What do you think the reading is probably about?

   _____

   _____

5. Read the first sentence in each paragraph. Now what do you think the reading is about?

   _____

   _____

Reading Passage

Conversational Ball Games

by Nancy Masterson Sakamoto
from *Polite Fictions—Why Japanese and Americans Seem Rude to Each Other*

1　After I was married and had lived in **Japan** for a while, my Japanese gradually improved to the point where I could take part in simple conversations with my husband and his friends and family. And I began to notice that often, when I joined in, the others would look
5　startled, and the conversational topic would come to a halt.[1] After this happened several times, it became clear to me that I was doing something wrong. But for a long time, I didn't know what it was.

　Finally, after listening carefully to many Japanese conversations, I discovered what my problem was. Even though I was speaking
10　Japanese, I was handling the conversation[2] in a **Western** way.

　Japanese-style conversations develop quite differently from Western-style conversations. And the difference isn't only in the languages. I realized that just as I kept trying to hold Western-style conversations even when I was speaking Japanese, so my English students kept trying to hold
15　Japanese-style conversations even when they were speaking English. We were unconsciously playing entirely different conversational ball games.

　A Western-style conversation between two people is like a game of tennis. If I introduce a topic,[3] a conversational ball, I expect you to hit it back. If you agree with me, I don't expect you simply to agree and do
20　nothing more. I expect you to add something—a reason for agreeing, another example, or an elaboration[4] to carry the idea further. But I don't expect you always to agree. I am just as happy if you question me, or challenge me, or completely disagree with me. Whether you agree or disagree, your response will return the ball to me.[5]

Map page 162

25　And then it is my turn again. I don't serve a new ball from my original starting line. I hit your ball back again from where it has bounced.[6] I carry your idea further, or answer your questions or objections, or challenge or question you. And so the ball goes back and forth.

Culture and
Language Notes
page 152

1　**come to a halt**　stop
2　**handling the conversation**　participating in the conversation
3　**introduce a topic**　begin talking about something
4　**elaboration**　extra detail
5　**return the ball to me**　allow me to continue the conversation
6　**bounce**　hit the ground and go up again

If there are more than two people in the conversation, then it is like
doubles in tennis, or like **volleyball**. There's no waiting in line. Whoever is
nearest and quickest hits the ball, and if you step back, someone else will
hit it. No one stops the game to give you a turn.[7] You're responsible for
taking your own turn.

But whether it's two players or a group, everyone does his or her best to
keep the ball going, and no one person has the ball for very long.

A Japanese-style conversation, however, is not at all like tennis or
volleyball. It's like **bowling**. You wait for your turn. And you always know
your place in line. It depends on such things as whether you are older or
younger, a close friend or a relative stranger[8] to the previous speaker, in
a senior or junior position, and so on.

When your turn comes, you step up to the starting line with your
bowling ball and carefully bowl it. Everyone else stands back and watches
politely, murmuring encouragement.[9] Everyone waits until the ball has
reached the end of the alley and watches to see if it knocks down all the
pins, or only some of them, or none of them. There is a pause, while
everyone registers[10] your score.

Then, after everyone is sure that you have completely finished your
turn, the next person in line steps up to the same starting line, with a
different ball. He doesn't return your ball, and he does not begin from
where your ball stopped. And there is always a suitable pause between
turns. There is no rush, no scramble[11] for the ball.

No wonder[12] everyone looked startled when I took part in Japanese
conversations. I paid no attention to whose turn it was and kept snatching
the ball[13] halfway down the alley and throwing it back at the bowler. Of
course the conversation died. I was playing the wrong game.

But if you have been trained all your life to play one game, it is no
simple matter to switch to another, even if you know the rules. Knowing
the rules is not at all the same thing as playing the game.

---

[7] **give you a turn**   give you a chance to play

[8] **a relative stranger**   someone you don't know very well

[9] **murmuring encouragement**   giving encouragement in a soft voice

[10] **registers**   writes down on an official form

[11] **no scramble**   no competition; no fighting

[12] **no wonder**   It's not surprising

[13] **snatching the ball**   quickly taking the ball from someone else

Even now, during a conversation in Japanese, I will notice a startled
60 reaction and belatedly realize[14] that once again I have rudely interrupted
by instinctively trying to hit back the other person's bowling ball. It is
no easier for me to "just listen" during a conversation than it is for my
Japanese students to "just relax" when speaking with foreigners. Now I
can truly sympathize with how hard they must find it to try to carry on
65 a Western-style conversation.[15]

Word Count: 779   Reading Time: _____   Words per Minute: _____
(Minutes)   (Word Count/Reading Time)

About the Author

American Nancy Sakamoto wrote "Conversational Ball Games" while she was
teaching English in Japan. She wrote about other experiences and cross-cultural
observations of her life in Japan in a book called *Polite Fictions: Why Japanese
and Americans Seem Rude to Each Other.*

After You Read
Understanding the Text

A. Comprehension
For each item below, fill in the correct circle.

1. **Finding the Main Idea** The main idea of this article is:
   Ⓐ People converse differently in Japan than in the West.
   Ⓑ It's important to take part in conversations.
   Ⓒ It's difficult to have a conversation with someone from another country.
   Ⓓ It's rude to interrupt someone who is speaking.

2. **Scanning for Details** The author makes all of the following arguments except:
   Ⓐ Japanese-style conversations are like bowling.
   Ⓑ Western-style conversations are like tennis or volleyball.
   Ⓒ In Japanese-style conversations, you must wait your turn to speak.
   Ⓓ Western-style conversations are longer than Japanese-style
      conversations.

---

[14] **belatedly realize**   realize after it's too late
[15] **carry on a conversation**   have a conversation

3. **Using Context** In line 44, the word *alley* probably means ___ in bowling.
   - (A) the place where you write your score
   - (B) the place where players sit
   - (C) something you wear
   - (D) the place where you roll the ball

4. **Identifying Pronoun References** In line 6, the word *this* refers to:
   - (A) I had simple conversations with my friends.
   - (B) People looked surprised when I said something in Japanese.
   - (C) My Japanese became good enough for me to have conversations with Japanese friends.
   - (D) When I joined the conversation, people looked surprised and the conversation stopped.

5. **Making Inferences** You can infer from the article that the author ___.
   - (A) was born in Japan
   - (B) has always lived in Japan
   - (C) is a teacher
   - (D) no longer lives in Japan

6. **Identifying the Author's Purpose** The author's purpose in writing this article was not to ___.
   - (A) instruct
   - (B) entertain
   - (C) compare
   - (D) criticize

B. Consider the Issues

Work with a partner to answer the questions below.

1. What are the characteristics of a Western-style conversation and a Japanese-style conversation? Add ideas from the article to the chart below.

Western Conversation	Japanese Conversation
okay to disagree	important to wait for your turn to speak

2. When you are having a conversation with a friend, is it more like a Western-style or a Japanese-style conversation? Why?

3. What is the author's attitude toward Western- and Japanese-style conversations? Does she think one style is better than the other?

Building Vocabulary

Learning Prefixes

You can add a prefix to certain words to add the meaning *not* to the word. For example, the word *unconscious* means *not conscious*.

Prefixes that mean *not*:

un-   in-   ir-   ab-   dis-   im-

A. Add a prefix from the box to each boldfaced word below to add the meaning *not*.

1. an **expected** answer   *an unexpected answer*

2. a **responsible** person   _____

3. a **suitable** pause   _____

4. a **motivated** student   _____

5. a **supportive** group   _____

6. a **successful** team   _____

7. a **normal** request   _____

8. an **effective** way to study   _____

9. **similar** interests   _____

10. an **agreeable** person   _____

11. a **polite** remark   _____

B. Look in a dictionary to find three more examples of adjectives with these prefixes meaning *not* and write them in the chart below.

un____	in____	ir____
unpopular	incomplete	irreversible

Reading Skill

Understanding Patterns of Organization
As you read, it's helpful to understand how the ideas in a piece of writing are organized. Below are three commonly-used organizational patterns in English.

Organized by time. When writers tell a story, they often present the events in the story in the order in which they happened. Dates and time phrases (*in the morning; when I was 16*) indicate that the writing is organized by time.

Organized by order of importance. When writers want to explain something, they may provide reasons or examples starting with the most important information and ending with the least important. Alternatively, they may start with the least important information and end with the most important.

Organized by similarities or differences. When writers want to show how two things are similar or different, they can first describe one thing in detail and then go on to describe the other thing. Alternatively, they can say something short about one thing and then immediately say how the second thing is similar or different.

A. Apply the Reading Skill
Look back at the readings listed below and identify the general pattern of organization. Write *Time, Order of Importance,* or *Differences.*

Title of Reading	Organizational Pattern
1. Conversational Ball Games (page 93)	_____
2. Answering 6 Common Interview Questions (page 3)	_____
3. Student Learning Teams (page 23)	_____
4. Culture Shock (page 53)	_____
5. Private Lives (page 63)	_____

Understanding Figurative Language

Writers use figurative language to help readers visualize something or see something in a new way. One way writers do this is by making an unusual comparison between two different things that have something in common. For example, in the reading on pages 93–95, the writer compares a Western-style conversation to a game of tennis.

Sometimes writers make comparisons directly by using words such as *like*, *as*, or *resemble*.

Examples

A Western-style conversation between two people is **like** a game of tennis.

If there are more than two people in the conversation, then it is **like** doubles in tennis, or **like** volleyball.

B. Apply the Reading Skill

Read the sentences from previous readings below and answer the questions.

1. There is a tiny slice of the Gulf of Mexico that belongs to me. Looking across the water, or down the shoreline, I see the past 20 years play over and over, like an old Super 8 movie.

   a. What two things is the writer comparing?

   b. Do you think this is an effective comparison? Why or why not?

2. I go to my beach not only to relax and think, but also to feed off the sea. The waves are gentle, the water soothing. But more important to me is the sea's permanence and sheer force. I want to be strong like that.

   a. What two things is the writer comparing?

   b. Do you think this is an effective comparison? Why or why not?

3. The pressing problem for Blackmore was making a quick adjustment to the American lifestyle that felt like it was run by a stopwatch. For this easygoing Australian, Americans seemed like perpetual-motion machines.

   a. What two things is the writer comparing?

   b. Do you think this is an effective comparison? Why or why not?

4. "BC students and faculty are like one big happy family," she says. "There is a real sense of team spirit."

   a. What two things is the writer comparing?

   b. Do you think this is an effective comparison? Why or why not?

Discussion & Writing

1. Is the conversation below a Japanese-style conversation or a Western-style conversation? Why do you think so?

   Paul: What did you think of the movie?

   Susan: I thought it was great—especially the ending.

   Paul: Really? Didn't you think it was sad?

   Susan: Well, a little bit, but it was funny, too.

   Paul: What do you mean?

   Susan: …

2. What could you say to keep the conversation below going Western-style? In the boxes below, write three possible responses to John's statement.

   John: Australia is the best place to go on vacation.

1. Agree and then add something.	2. Ask a question.	3. Disagree and add something.

3. Complete the opinions below. Then read one of your opinions to a partner and see how long you can keep a Western-style conversation going. Take turns until you have discussed each opinion.

   a. I think _____ is a really good movie.

   b. _____ is a great place for a vacation.

   c. I think it's dangerous to _____ .

   d. _____ (your own idea)

Mini-Dictionary page 163

Words to Remember		
NOUNS	**VERBS**	**ADJECTIVES**
attention	expect	further
encouragement	handle	original
matter	improve	previous
pause	interrupt	simple
response	notice	suitable
	register	
	train	

Letters of Application

Chapter Focus

CONTENT
Applying for a job

READING SKILL
Notetaking

BUILDING VOCABULARY
Understanding
connecting words

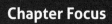

"An interview opens the door; a letter of application rings the doorbell."

— Anonymous

Before You Read

A. **Connect with the topic.** When people apply for a job, they often send a letter of application to the employer. What do you know about letters of application? Check (✓)True or False for each statement.

	True	False
1. The reason for writing a letter of application is to get a job interview.	☐	☐
2. When sending a letter of application you must always send a résumé,[1] too.	☐	☐
3. It's a good idea to talk about your best qualities and biggest accomplishments in a letter of application.	☐	☐
4. You should mention the salary you want in a letter of application.	☐	☐

B. **Pair work.** Have you ever had a job? How did you get your job? Compare your experiences with a partner.

C. **Preview the reading.** Look quickly over the reading on pages 103–105 to complete the Previewing Chart below.

Previewing Chart

1. Title of the reading: _____

2. Key words. (What words appear several times? List 3 more.)

letter   _____

_____   _____

3. Read the first sentence in each paragraph. What do you think the reading is probably about?

_____

_____

4. Read the first paragraph. What questions do you have about letters of application? (Write 2 questions.)

_____?

_____?

---

[1] **résumé** one- or two-page summary of your education and work experience

Letters of Application

by Andrea B. Geffner
from *Business Letters the Easy Way*

1   A **letter of application** is a sales letter in which you are both salesperson and product, for the purpose of an application is to attract an employer's attention and persuade him or her to grant you an interview.[2] To do this, the letter presents what you can offer the
5   employer, rather than what you want from the job.

Like a **résumé**, the letter of application is a sample of your work; and it is, as well, an opportunity to demonstrate, not just talk about, your skills and personality. If it is written with flair[3] and understanding and prepared with professional care, it is likely to hit its mark.[4]

10   There are two types of application letters. A *solicited* letter (see page 110) is sent in response to a **help-wanted ad**. Because such a letter will be in competition with many, perhaps several hundred others, it must be composed with distinction.[5] At the same time, it must refer to the ad and the specific job advertised.

15   An *unsolicited* letter is sent to a company for which you would like to work though you know of no particular opening. The advantage of this type of application, however, is that there will be little competition and you can define yourself the position you would like to apply for. You can send out as many letters as you wish, to as many companies as you
20   are aware of; it is a good idea, though, to find out the name of a specific person to whom you can send the letter—a more effective approach than simply addressing the letter to "**Personnel**."

Because a letter of application must sell your qualifications,[6] it must do more than simply restate your résumé in paragraph form. While the
25   résumé must be factual, objective, and brief, the letter is your chance to interpret and expand. It should state explicitly how your background relates to the specific job, and it should emphasize your strongest and most pertinent characteristics. The letter should demonstrate that you know both yourself and the company.

Culture and Language Notes page 153

---

2   **grant you an interview**   schedule an interview with you
3   **written with flair**   written with special skill and style
4   **hit the mark**   be very effective
5   **composed with distinction**   written extremely well
6   **sell your qualifications**   present your skills and abilities in the best way

30   A letter of application must communicate your ambition and
      enthusiasm. Yet it must, at the same time, be modest. It should be
      neither aggressive nor meek: neither pat yourself on the back[7] nor ask
      for sympathy. It should never express dissatisfaction with a present or
      former job or employer. And you should avoid discussing your reasons
35   for leaving your last job.

      Keep in mind the following principles when writing your letter of
      application:

      1. *Start by attracting attention.* You must say, of course, that you are
      applying and mention both the specific job and how you heard about it.
40   But try to avoid a mundane opening.[8] Instead of:

      *I would like to apply for the position of legal secretary, which you
      advertised in the* Los Angeles Times *of Sunday, August 10…*

      Try something a bit more original:

      *I believe you will find my experiences in the Alameda **District Attorney's***
45   *office have prepared me well for the position of legal secretary, which you
      advertised in the* Los Angeles Times *of Sunday, August 10…*

      2. *Continue by describing your qualifications.* Highlight your strengths and
      achievements and say how they suit you for the job at hand.[9] Provide
      details and explanations not found on your résumé, and refer the
50   reader to the résumé for the remaining, less pertinent facts.

      3. *Assure the employer that you are the person for the job.* List verifiable
      facts[10] that prove you are not exaggerating or lying. Mention the names
      of any familiar or prominent **references** you may have. In some way,
      distinguish yourself from the mass of other qualified applicants.[11]

55   **4.** *Conclude by requesting an interview.* Urge the employer to action by
      making it easy to contact you. Mention your telephone number and
      the best hours to reach you, or state that you will call him or her within
      a few days.

      A complete application should contain both a letter of application and
60   a résumé. While it is possible to write a letter so complete in detail that a
      résumé seems redundant,[12] it is always most professional to include both.

---

7 **pat yourself on the back**   give yourself credit for your accomplishments
8 **mundane opening**   boring or unoriginal introduction
9 **the job at hand**   the work to be done
10 **verifiable facts**   professional information that someone can easily check
11 **mass of other qualified applicants**   all of the other qualified people who applied for the job
12 **redundant**   unnecessary because it repeats the same information

Finally, a word about salary: basically, unless instructed by the want ad, it is best that you not broach the subject.[13] Indeed, even if an ad requires that you mention your salary requirements, it is advisable simply to
65 call them "negotiable."[14] However, when you go on and interview, you should be prepared to mention a salary range (e.g., $40,000–$45,000). For this reason, you should investigate both your field, and, if possible, the particular company. You don't want to ask for less than you deserve or more than is reasonable.

 Word Count: 896

| Reading Time: _____ | Words per Minute: _____ |
| (Minutes) | (Word Count/Reading Time) |

About the Author

Andrea B. Geffner is a business educator and writer. She is the former dean of the Taylor Business Institute in New York.

After You Read
Understanding the Text

A. Comprehension
For each item below, fill in the correct circle.

1. **Identifying the Author's Purpose** The main purpose of this reading is to ____.

   Ⓐ show people how to write effective letters of application

   Ⓑ help people find interesting jobs

   Ⓒ explain the differences between a résumé and a letter of application

   Ⓓ explain how to have a good job interview

2. **Scanning for Details** A letter written in response to a help-wanted ad is ____.

   Ⓐ an unsolicited letter

   Ⓑ a solicited letter

   Ⓒ a reference letter

   Ⓓ a résumé

---

[13] **broach the subject** introduce the subject

[14] **negotiable** something that can be changed after discussion

3. **Scanning for Details** A letter of application should ___ the information contained in a résumé.

    Ⓐ restate   Ⓒ expand upon

    Ⓑ not address   Ⓓ analyze

4. **Using Context** *Pertinent characteristics* in line 28 is closest in meaning to ___.

    Ⓐ qualities you used to have   Ⓒ unusual qualities

    Ⓑ interesting qualities   Ⓓ qualities that are directly related to the job

5. **Understanding Tone** The overall tone of this reading is ___.

    Ⓐ light and informative   Ⓒ personal and informal

    Ⓑ serious and informative   Ⓓ entertaining

B. Consider the Issues

Work with a partner to answer the questions below.

1. According to the author, what are the things you should and shouldn't do when writing a letter of application? Fill in the chart with ideas from the article. Then add two ideas of your own to each column.

Should	Shouldn't
be original	
Your idea:	Your idea:
Your idea:	Your idea:

2. It's good to know some information about a company before you write a letter of application. What are three ways you can gather information on a company?

3. Why is it important not to express dissatisfaction with a former job or employer in a letter of application or on an interview?

Building Vocabulary

Understanding Connecting Words

As you learned in Chapter 4, connecting words signal the type of information that is coming next. We also use connecting words to show relationships between phrases or sentences. Each connecting word has a specific purpose.

Purpose	Connecting Words	Example
add new information	also and in addition to	**In addition to** my administrative duties, I was responsible for scheduling all of Ms. Jenkins' appointments.
compare and contrast	but yet however	A letter of application must communicate your ambition and enthusiasm. **Yet**, it must, at the same time, be modest.
show a result	therefore thus	I did everything I could to make Ms. Jenkins' heavy responsibilities easier. **Thus**, I am familiar with the duties of an executive assistant.

A. Look back at the reading on pages 103–105. Circle one example of these connecting words: *and*, *but*, *yet*, and *however*.

B. Use a connecting word from the chart above to complete each sentence below. More than one answer is possible.

1. John was nervous about his interview. _____, he began to feel confident after reading a book about how to prepare for an interview.

2. John knew he couldn't wear his usual casual jeans and T-shirt to the interview. _____, he went out and bought a suit.

3. Looking very professional in his new suit, John made sure to arrive at the interview early. _____, he was able to make a good first impression.

4. John did some research about the company before his interview. _____, he practiced answering questions he thought the interviewer might ask.

5. The interviewer was a very important person in the company. _____, he had a warm and friendly smile that put John at ease.

Reading Skill

Notetaking

Taking notes on a reading helps you to remember and study the information. Good notes are always short and clear. They should help you to remember something without confusing you later. Follow these tips for taking good notes:

1. Write down only the most important ideas. Look for:
   - bold, italicized, or underlined words.
   - headings or subheadings.
   - information that is repeated.
2. Don't write complete sentences.
3. Abbreviate words (*president = pres*, *you are = u r*) and use symbols (+, −, =, <).
4. Use bulleted lists.

A. Analyze the Reading

The notes below are based on the reading on pages 103–105. Write *E* (for effective) or *I* (for ineffective) next to each note. Then explain why the note is effective or ineffective.

Main Idea	Why E or I?
1. _____ let of app ➝ job intvw	_____
Supporting Ideas	
2. _____ Like a résumé, the letter of application is a sample of your work; and it is, as well, an opportunity to demonstrate, not just talk about, your skills and personality.	_____
3. _____ application letter = sales letter	_____
4. _____ would like to apply for position of legal secretary	_____
5. _____ • Use original opening • Describe qualif. • Assure emplyr u r person for job • Request intvw	_____

B. Apply the Reading Skill

Read the selection below and take notes. Use the notetaking rules you have learned.

After a Job Interview

by Peggy Schmidt
from *The 90-Minute Interview Prep Book*

This section provides some guidelines that will help you end a good job interview.

Before You Leave the Interview

- Thank the interviewer for the opportunity to meet with him or her. Mention your interest in the job and the company.
- Ask about the company's time frame for making a hiring decision.
- Ask if it's all right for you to call back in a week's time to check where things stand.[15]

Interview Follow-Up

Writing a note to the person or people with whom you interviewed is an incredibly simple but important idea. And it can make the difference in getting hired.

1. Type the letter; it's more professional-looking.

2. Thank the interviewer for talking to you. Mention something he or she said that was particularly interesting to you.

3. Explain in a sentence or two why you think you are a good match for the job or company. Be specific about what you think you can do for the company.

4. Conclude your letter by saying you hope to get the job and that you are happy to answer any additional questions that the interviewer has for you.

Main Idea

Supporting Ideas

---

[15] **check where things stand**   see if the company has made a decision to hire anyone

Discussion & Writing

1. You are going to write a letter of application for a job you would like to have. Complete the chart. Your qualifications can be real or imagined.

Name of the job:
My qualifications:
1. _____
2. _____
3. _____
4. _____

2. Write a letter of application. Use your ideas in the chart above and the advice in the reading on pages 103–105.

Example

Dear Ms. Martinez,

Having served for the past several years as the administrative assistant for a private business, I would like to apply for the position of executive assistant which you advertised on the AssistantJobs.com website on Sunday, February 28.

As administrative assistant at the Benlow Corporation in Chicago, I was directly responsible to Alba Jenkins, the company's owner. In addition to my administrative duties, I was responsible for…

Mini-Dictionary
page 163

Words to Remember

NOUNS	VERBS	ADJECTIVES
advantage	assure	aggressive
ambition	contain	aware
approach	deserve	brief
characteristic	exaggerate	reasonable
competition	expand	
enthusiasm	grant	
mass	highlight	
objective	mention	
principle	refer	

Out to Lunch

"Take a step back, evaluate what is important, and enjoy life."

— Teri Garr, American actress (1944–)

Before You Read

A. **Connect with the topic.** In some countries, businesses and schools close for several hours in the middle of the day so that people can go home to eat and relax. What do you think are the advantages and disadvantages of this custom? List your ideas in the chart below.

Advantages	Disadvantages
You have more time to spend with your family.	

B. **Pair work.** Compare charts with a partner. How many of your ideas were the same?

C. **Preview the reading.** Skim the reading on pages 113–115 to complete the Previewing Chart below.

Previewing Chart

1. Title of the reading: _____

2. Names of people and places in the reading. (List 3 more.)

   Europe _____

   _____ _____

3. Key words. (What words appear several times? List 3 more.)

   nap _____

   _____ _____

4. Read the first sentence in each paragraph. What do you think the reading is probably about?

   _____

   _____

   _____

Reading Passage

Out To Lunch

by Joe Robinson
from *Escape* magazine

1   *A big meal and a long nap is still a way of life in Madrid.*

Birds do it. Cats do it. And Spaniards most especially do it—every day, in broad daylight. They nap. Grown adults—executives, teachers, civil servants[1]—wink off[2] in the middle of the workday. From 1 or 2 o'clock
5   to 4:30 or so every afternoon, **Spain** stops the world for a stroll home, a leisurely meal, and a few z's.[3] **Common Market** technocrats[4] have informed the Spanish that this is not the way things will get done in a unified Europe.

At a time when productivity is the world's largest religion, the **siesta**
10   tradition lives on.[5] In Spain, work operates under the command of life,[6] instead of the other way around. No task is so critical that it can't wait a couple of hours while you attend to[7] more important matters like eating, relaxing, or catching up on sleep. When the midday break hits, offices empty and streets clear. Befuddled foreigners quickly learn that they have
15   entered a new circadian order.[8]

 Map page 159

Culture and
Language Notes
page 154

---

[1] **civil servants**   government employees

[2] **wink off**   go to sleep

[3] **a few z's**   a nap; a short sleep

[4] **technocrats**   government experts in science and technology

[5] **lives on**   continues

[6] **work operates under the command of life**   working is less important than living

[7] **attend to**   take care of; do

[8] **a new circadian order**   a new way of organizing sleep and wake patterns

113

"At first, I kept looking for things to do in the afternoon, and I just couldn't believe that nothing was open," recalls Pier Roberts, an Oakland writer who lived in Spain for several years. "I walked the streets of **Madrid** looking for somewhere to go. It was a thousand degrees[9] outside, you could see the heat waves, and it was like a ghost town."[10]

Taking a long break in the middle of the day is not only healthier than the conventional lunch, it's apparently more natural. Sleep researchers have found that the Spanish biorhythm[11] may be tuned more closely to our biological clocks.[12] Studies suggest that humans are "biphasic" creatures, requiring days broken up by two periods of sleep instead of one "monophasic" shift. The drowsiness you feel after lunch comes not from the food but from the time of day.

"All animals, including humans, have a biological rhythm," explains Claudio Stampi, director of the Chrono Biology Research Institute in Newton, Massachusetts. "One is a 24-hour rhythm—we get tired by the end of the day and go to sleep—and there is a secondary peak of sleepiness and a decrease in alertness in the early afternoon. Some people have difficulty remaining awake, doing any sort of task between one and four in the afternoon. For others it's less difficult, but it's there. So there is a biological reason for siestas."

Unlike the average lunch break, the siesta is a true break in the action because there is no choice but to come to a full and complete stop. You can't do errands; the shops are closed. You can't make business calls; nobody's at the office. Most people go home for lunch, or get together with family or friends and nod out[13] afterwards.

The Spanish need their sleep. They've got a long night ahead of them because another key component of the siesta lifestyle is its nocturnal orbit.[14] After the afternoon work shift, from 4:30 to 8 p.m. or so, they may join friends for a drink. Dinner starts at 9 or 10 p.m., and from there it's out on the town[15] until one or two in the morning.

"It's a bad night in Madrid if you get home before six in the morning," laughs Roberts. The siesta's origins lie in climate and architecture. Like people in other places around the globe that are blast furnaces[16] much of

---

9 **a thousand degrees**   extremely hot
10 **a ghost town**   an empty town; a town without people
11 **biorhythm**   rhythm of life
12 **biological clocks**   natural body rhythms
13 **nod out**   go to sleep
14 **nocturnal orbit**   nighttime activity
15 **out on the town**   having fun in town
16 **blast furnaces**   very hot places

the year, Spaniards turned to shade and stillness to avoid incineration[17]
50 in the middle of the day. At night, packed, simmering dwellings drove
people into the streets to cool down.

While climate is still a factor, the siesta lifestyle today is driven
primarily by the social imperative[18] of Spanish life, which places an equal,
if not greater, emphasis on life outside the office. "We are not so obsessed
55 only with work," says Florentino Sotomayor of the Spanish Tourist Board.
"We take a break and have the opportunity of having coffee with friends
and thinking and talking about different issues, not only work."

Word Count: 661   Reading Time: _____   Words per Minute: _____
                      (Minutes)   (Word Count/Reading Time)

About the Source

Escape magazine, published in Santa Monica, California, features a wide range
of advice and feature articles for the adventurous traveler. It focuses on unusual
vacations to out-of-the-way places, eco-tourism, and outdoor adventure.

After You Read
Understanding the Text

A. Comprehension
For each item below, fill in the correct circle.

1. **Finding the Main Idea** The main idea of this article is that ____.
   - Ⓐ people everywhere should take naps
   - Ⓑ napping is an important tradition in Spain
   - Ⓒ it is important to have traditions
   - Ⓓ the nightlife is exciting in Spain

2. **Finding the Main Idea** The main idea of paragraph 4 is that ____.
   - Ⓐ it's okay to feel sleepy in the middle of the day
   - Ⓑ all animals have biological clocks
   - Ⓒ food makes you feel drowsy
   - Ⓓ it's natural and healthy for humans to nap

---

[17] **incineration** burning up
[18] **social imperative** society's demands

3. **Scanning for Details** During the midday break in Spain, people ____.

    Ⓐ go home for lunch   Ⓒ make business calls

    Ⓑ do errands   Ⓓ go shopping

4. **Scanning for Details** A biphasic creature needs ____.

    Ⓐ two periods of sleep per day   Ⓒ two days of sleep

    Ⓑ eight hours of sleep per day   Ⓓ a long night of sleep

5. **Using Context** The word *peak* in line 31 is closest in meaning to ____.

    Ⓐ high point   Ⓒ cause

    Ⓑ mountain top   Ⓓ decrease

6. **Making Inferences** You can infer from the article that some businesspeople in other European countries ____.

    Ⓐ hope the siesta tradition will be introduced in their countries

    Ⓑ think that the siesta tradition is impractical

    Ⓒ think that the siesta tradition will grow in popularity

    Ⓓ don't agree that napping is good for you

7. **Identifying Pronoun References** In paragraph 1, the word *this* refers to ____.

    Ⓐ eating quickly   Ⓒ going home for lunch and a nap

    Ⓑ joining the Common Market   Ⓓ sleeping at night

8. **Understanding Tone** The overall tone of this article is ____.

    Ⓐ serious and academic   Ⓒ light and informative

    Ⓑ light and silly   Ⓓ scientific and technical

B. Consider the Issues

Work with a partner to answer the questions below.

1. According to the article, what are the advantages of the siesta?

2. In line 9, the writer claims that "productivity is the world's largest religion." What do you think he means by this? Do you agree? Why or why not?

3. Each of the statements below is an exaggeration of the truth. What is an exaggeration of the truth? Why do you think the author exaggerates the truth?

    • It was a thousand degrees outside.

    • It's a bad night in Madrid if you get home before six in the morning.

Building Vocabulary

> **Learning Word Forms**
> When you learn a new word, you can easily expand your vocabulary by learning other forms of the same word. For example, the noun form of the verb *emphasize* is *emphasis*. You can find different forms of a word in a dictionary.

A. Scan the reading on pages 113–115 to add the missing words to the chart below.

Noun	Verb	Adjective
1. information		informative
2.	produce	productive
3. suggestion		suggestive
4.	drowse	drowsy
5.	sleep	sleepy
6.	alert	alert
7.		difficult
8. leisure		

B. Now use a word from the chart above to complete each sentence below.

1. One of the most _____ articles I ever read on the subject appeared in the *Japan Times*.

2. Some researchers think that people would be more _____ if they took a nap during the day.

3. Do you have any _____ on how to improve my speech?

4. Hot weather can give you a headache and make you feel _____.

5. If you suffer from excessive _____ during the winter, you may need to get more sunlight.

6. I feel sleepy in the morning, but around 4 p.m. I start to feel _____.

7. Some people don't have any _____ with new technology; it seems easy for them.

8. I had such a stressful morning that I'm in need of a _____ lunch.

Reading Skill

Summarizing

When you summarize a piece of writing, you use your own words to express the *main points* in the text. A summary is always shorter than the original text.

When you write a summary:

- Focus on the main points in the reading.
- Don't include details or examples.
- Use your own words.
- Keep the author's viewpoint.

Hint! You might need to create the topic sentence for your summary from a combination of several points in the original.

A. Analyze the Reading

The ideas below are from the reading on pages 113–115. Write *M* next to the main points. Write *D* next to the details.

____ **1.** In Spain, your life is more important than your job.

____ **2.** The siesta starts at 1 or 2 o'clock and lasts until 4:30.

____ **3.** Everything closes during the siesta; you can't do business.

____ **4.** If you feel drowsy in the afternoon, it's because of the time of day.

____ **5.** Taking a noontime break is healthy and natural.

____ **6.** The hot climate in places like Spain gave rise to the siesta tradition.

____ **7.** In Spain, people stay out very late.

____ **8.** Most people don't have dinner until 9 or 10 p.m.

B. Evaluate the Reading Skill

Read this summary of the reading and answer the questions below.

> Everyday from 1 or 2 o'clock to 4:30, the people in Spain stop the world for a stroll home, a leisurely meal, and a few z's. In Spain, the siesta tradition lives on. Taking a long break in the middle of the day is healthier and more natural than the conventional lunch. Claudio Stampi says that all animals, including humans, have a biological rhythm.

1. Does the summary include all of the main points in the reading?

2. Did the writer of the summary use his own words?

3. Did the writer include any unnecessary details or examples?

C. Apply the Reading Skill

Read the paragraph below and identify the writer's main points. Then write a short summary of the paragraph.

A few years ago, I was sent by my company to work in Abu Dhabi. I really didn't know very much about the place. When I first arrived, I noticed two things that I thought were very different from the United States. First, the working week is different. It begins on Sunday, and the weekend is Friday and Saturday. In the U.S., the working week is Monday through Friday. At first it was hard to get up early for work on Sunday—I wanted to sleep late that day! Another difference that I noticed in Abu Dhabi is that services like housecleaning and laundry are very affordable. For example, most people I met have maids. This really surprised me. Back in the U.S., these services are quite expensive, and I am used to doing these things myself.

Main Points
•
•
•

Summary

Discussion & Writing

1. Group work. Traditions give information about values, or what people believe is important. What do you think these traditions say about values?

- In Spain, it's a tradition to take a long lunch break so you can have a leisurely lunch with your family and take a nap.
- In Turkey, it's a custom to take your shoes off before you enter a house.
- In the United States, it's a tradition for people to give flowers on birthdays, anniversaries, and other special occasions.

2. Work with your group to answer the questions below. Then share your answers with the class.

- What is one of your culture's most important traditions? What does it say about your culture's values?
- When you were a child, what was one of your favorite holiday traditions? Why did you like it?
- What do these two quotations mean to you?

"A tradition without intelligence is not worth having."
—T.S. Eliot, British writer (1888–1965)

"Tradition is a guide and not a jailer."
—W. Somerset Maugham, British writer (1874–1965)

Mini-Dictionary page 163

Words to Remember		
NOUNS	**VERBS**	**ADJECTIVES**
command	include	average
difficulty	inform	complete
emphasis	operate	conventional
factor	remain	critical
origins	require	key
shift		
task		
tradition		

Public Attitudes Toward Science

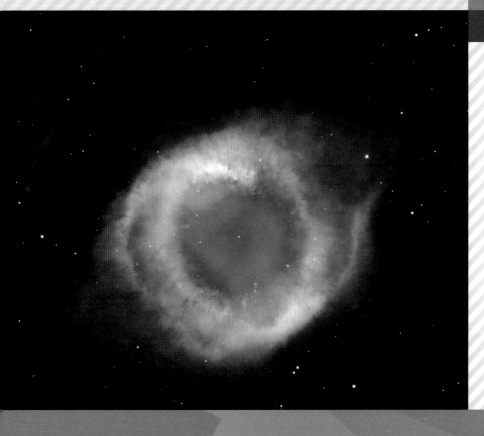

CONTENT
Talking about the importance of science

READING SKILL
Recognizing paragraph transitions

BUILDING VOCABULARY
Learning antonyms

"The most beautiful thing we can experience is the mysterious. It is the source of all true art and science."

— Albert Einstein, German-American physicist (1879–1955)

Before You Read

A. **Connect with the topic.** Which of the following methods have you used to learn about science-related topics? Check (✓) yes or no.

	Yes	No
1. memorize facts	☐	☐
2. watch TV documentaries about science	☐	☐
3. go to a science museum	☐	☐
4. read newspaper or magazine articles about science	☐	☐
5. read science fiction novels	☐	☐
6. do science experiments	☐	☐

B. **Pair work.** Talk about these questions with a partner.

1. Look at the list in Activity A. Which do you think is the best way to learn about science? Which do you think is the worst? Why?

2. Are you interested in science? If so, which areas of science interest you the most?

3. Are you interested in science fiction? If so, what are your favorite science fiction books or movies? If not, why not?

C. **Preview the reading.** Skim the reading on pages 123–125 to complete the Previewing Chart below.

Previewing Chart

1. Title of the reading: _____

2. Key words. (What words appear several times? List 3 more.)

   <u>change</u>

   _____

   _____

   _____

3. Read the first sentence in each paragraph. What do you think the reading is probably about?

_____

_____

_____

Reading Passage

Public Attitudes Toward Science

by Stephen Hawking
from *Black Holes and Baby Universes and Other Essays*

1   Whether we like it or not, the world we live in has changed a great deal in the last hundred years, and it is likely to change even more in the next hundred. Some people would like to stop these changes and go back to what they see as a purer and simpler age. But as history

5   shows, the past was not that wonderful. It was not so bad for a privileged minority,[1] though even they had to do without modern medicine, and childbirth was highly risky for women. But for the vast majority of the population, life was nasty and short.

Anyway, even if one wanted to, one couldn't put the clock back to

10   an earlier age. Knowledge and techniques can't just be forgotten. Nor can one prevent further advances in the future. Even if all government money for research were cut off, the force of competition would still bring about advances in technology. Moreover, one cannot stop inquiring minds[2] from thinking about basic science, whether or not they were paid for it.

15   If we accept that we cannot prevent science and technology from changing our world, we can at least try to ensure that the changes they make are in the right directions. In a democratic society, this means that the public needs to have a basic understanding of science, so that it can make informed decisions and not leave them in the hands of experts. At

20   the moment, the public has a rather ambivalent attitude toward science.[3] It has come to expect the steady increase in the **standard of living** that new developments in science and technology have brought to continue, but it also distrusts science because it doesn't understand it. This distrust is evident in the cartoon figure of the mad scientist working in his

25   laboratory to produce a **Frankenstein**. But the public also has a great interest in science, as is shown by the large audiences for **science fiction**.

Culture and
Language Notes
page 155

---

[1] **privileged minority**   small group of lucky people
[2] **inquiring minds**   people who are very interested in a topic
[3] **ambivalent attitude toward science**   liking certain aspects of science and disliking others

What can be done to harness this interest[4] and give the public the scientific background it needs to make informed decisions on subjects like **acid rain**, the **greenhouse effect**, nuclear weapons, and **genetic**
30   **engineering**? Clearly, the basis must lie in what is taught in schools. But in schools science is often presented in a dry and uninteresting manner. Children must learn it by rote[5] to pass examinations, and they don't see its relevance to the world around them. Moreover, science is often taught in terms of equations. Although equations are a concise and accurate way of
35   describing mathematical ideas, they frighten most people.

Scientists and engineers tend to express their ideas in the form of equations because they need to know the precise value of quantities. But for the rest of us, a qualitative grasp of scientific concepts is sufficient, and this can be conveyed by words and diagrams, without the use of
40   equations.

The science people learn in school can provide the basic framework.[6] But the rate of scientific progress is now so rapid that there are always new developments that have occurred since one was at school or university. I never learned about **molecular biology** or transistors[7] at school, but
45   genetic engineering and computers are two of the developments most likely to change the way we live in the future. Popular books and magazine articles about science can help to put across new developments, but even the most successful popular book is read by only a small proportion of the population. There are some very good science programs on TV, but others
50   present scientific wonders simply as magic, without explaining them or showing how they fit into the framework of scientific ideas. Producers of television science programs should realize that they have a responsibility to educate the public, not just entertain it.

What are the science-related issues that the public will have to make
55   decisions on in the near future? By far the most urgent is that of nuclear weapons. Other global problems, such as food supply or the greenhouse effect, are relatively slow-acting, but a nuclear war could mean the end of all human life on earth within days. The relaxation of **East-West tensions** has meant that the fear of nuclear war has receded from public
60   consciousness.[8] But the danger is still there as long as there are enough weapons to kill the entire population of the world many times over.

---

4   **harness this interest**   use this interest
5   **learn by rote**   learn by repeating the same thing many times
6   **basic framework**   general facts and ideas on a topic
7   **transistors**   small electronic parts in radios and TVs
8   **receded from public consciousness**   left people's everyday thoughts

Nuclear weapons are still poised to strike[9] all the major cities in the Northern Hemisphere.[10] It would only take a computer error to trigger[11] a global war.

65   If we manage to avoid a nuclear war, there are still other dangers that could destroy us all. There's a sick joke[12] that the reason we have not been contacted by an alien civilization[13] is that civilizations tend to destroy themselves when they reach our stage.[14] But I have sufficient faith in the good sense of the public to believe that we might prove this wrong.

 Word Count: 821   Reading Time: _____   Words per Minute: _____
                                        (Minutes)   (Word Count/Reading Time)

About the Author

Stephen Hawking (1942–) is a physicist, professor at Cambridge University in England, and author of the award-winning book, *A Brief History of Time*. Hawking studies black holes, the big bang theory, and other scientific mysteries of the universe.

After You Read
Understanding the Text

A. Comprehension
For each item below, fill in the correct circle.

1. Finding the Main Idea The main idea of this reading is:

   Ⓐ The public should be educated about science so they can make good decisions.

   Ⓑ The media can educate people about the most recent developments in technology.

   Ⓒ The science people learn in school can provide a basic framework for scientific understanding.

   Ⓓ Many people don't trust science because they don't understand it.

---

9   **poised to strike**   ready to attack
10 **Northern Hemisphere**   the portion of Earth north of the Equator
11 **trigger**   start
12 **sick joke**   story that makes fun of serious topics like death
13 **alien civilization**   people from another planet
14 **our stage**   our level of scientific development

2. **Scanning for Details** History shows that in the past life was ____.
   Ⓐ not so bad
   Ⓑ comfortable for most people
   Ⓒ hard for most people
   Ⓓ easier for women

3. **Scanning for Details** The public feels ____.
   Ⓐ ambivalent toward science
   Ⓑ completely positive about science
   Ⓒ completely negative about science
   Ⓓ negative about science fiction

4. **Scanning for Details** Science programs on TV should ____.
   Ⓐ present a lot of equations
   Ⓑ focus on science fiction
   Ⓒ show science as a kind of magic
   Ⓓ educate the public, as well as entertain

5. **Using Context** The phrase *qualitative grasp of* in line 38 is closest in meaning to ____.
   Ⓐ detailed understanding of
   Ⓑ interest in
   Ⓒ general understanding of
   Ⓓ hold of

6. **Making Inferences** The author believes that ____.
   Ⓐ human civilization won't survive for more than a hundred more years
   Ⓑ only trained scientists can solve the world's problems
   Ⓒ the public will probably find ways to solve the world's biggest problems
   Ⓓ aliens from another planet will visit Earth someday

B. Consider the Issues

Work with a partner to answer the questions below.

1. According to the author, what are the reasons that many people don't like science? Do you agree with the reasons he gives? Why or why not?

2. According to the author, what are some of the ways people can educate themselves about scientific issues? Are they the same ways that you have used to learn about science?

3. The author writes, "The world has changed a great deal in the last hundred years, and it is likely to change even more in the next hundred." What are one or two scientific discoveries that you think will be made during your lifetime?

Building Vocabulary

A. Scan the reading on pages 123–125 to find antonyms for the following words.

1. safe (paragraph 1) _____
2. minority (paragraph 1) _____
3. ignorance (paragraph 2) _____
4. decrease (paragraph 3) _____
5. incorrect (paragraph 4) _____
6. approximate (paragraph 5) _____
7. slow (paragraph 6) _____
8. intensification (paragraph 7) _____
9. advance (paragraph 7) _____
10. create (paragraph 8) _____

B. Now use an answer from Activity A to complete each sentence below.

1. An _____ in government funding of the space program allowed astronomers to study Mars.

2. Many people fear that nuclear war will _____ human civilization.

3. Space travel is always _____, but the benefits are worth the danger that astronauts must face.

4. _____ about science will help the public to make informed decisions.

5. A few people wish for the days before scientific and technological advances, but the _____ appreciate the conveniences of the modern world.

Reading Skill

Recognizing Paragraph Transitions

Paragraph transitions connect the ideas in one paragraph to the ideas in the next paragraph. Writers often make a transition by repeating parts of an idea from the previous paragraph.

Example

Last Sentence/Paragraph 3:

...But the public also has *a great interest* in science, as is shown by the large audiences for science fiction.

First Sentence/Paragraph 4:

What can be done to harness *this interest* and give the public the scientific background it needs to make informed decisions on subjects like acid rain, the greenhouse effect, nuclear weapons, and genetic engineering?

A. Analyze the Reading

Circle the word(s) in the second paragraph that repeat the italicized idea from the first paragraph.

1. Middle of Paragraph 1:

...Some people would like to stop these changes and go back to what they see as *a purer and simpler age*. But as history shows, the past was not that wonderful.

First Sentence/Paragraph 2:

Anyway, even if one wanted to, one couldn't put the clock back to an earlier age.

2. Last Sentence/Paragraph 4:

...Moreover, science is often taught in *terms of equations*. Although equations are a concise and accurate way of describing mathematical ideas, they frighten most people.

First Sentence/Paragraph 5:

Scientists and engineers tend to express their ideas in the form of equations because they need to know the precise value of quantities.

3. Last Sentence/Paragraph 7:

...*Nuclear weapons* are still poised to strike all the major cities in the Northern Hemisphere. It would only take a computer error to trigger a *global war*.

First Sentence/Paragraph 8:

If we manage to avoid a nuclear war, there are still other dangers that could destroy us all.

B. Apply the Reading Skill

Fill in the blanks to make paragraph transitions. Circle the ideas from the previous paragraph that are repeated in your transition. Then add a comment giving your opinion on the topic.

Home   News   Business   Sports   Entertainment   Health   Blog   A&E/Living

The SciFi Guy Blog

Science fiction doesn't always get the respect it deserves. My friend Ryan calls it "brain candy." My sister says science fiction novels are fairy tales for teenagers. If you ask me, people think they shouldn't take science fiction seriously because it's so much fun to read.

Yes, science fiction is _____, but it's also "real" literature. After all, some of the greats of literature—Ray Bradbury, Isaac Asimov, Ursula Le Guin—have written science fiction.

Not only are science fiction books often examples of great _____, the predictions made by science fiction writers help spark people's imagination and lay the groundwork for inventions of the future.

One accurate _____ by a science fiction writer was the invention of the automatic sliding door, which H.G. Wells wrote about in *When the Sleeper Wakes* in 1899. The first automatic doors were invented in 1954. I wonder if the inventors got the idea from H.G. Wells?

Okay, so maybe we could survive without _____, but in his short story "From the *London Times* of 1904" (published in 1898), Mark Twain described a more significant invention—the Internet (specifically, video blogging)! Imagine what the world would be like without the Internet. Thank you, Mr. Twain. Thank you, science fiction!

Add a comment

Discussion & Writing

1. What is the most important invention of the past 50 years? Why is it important? In the chart, make notes about the invention you have chosen.

Name of the invention:
Why the invention is important:
1. _____
2. _____
3. _____
4. _____

2. **Group work.** Explain your ideas from question 1 to your group.

3. Write a summary of your group's ideas about the most important inventions of the past 50 years.

Mini-Dictionary
page 163

Words to Remember

NOUNS	VERBS	ADJECTIVES
attitude	avoid	accurate
background	destroy	basic
basis	manage	precise
development	prevent	pure
minority		rapid
progress		vast
proportion		
standard		
technique		

The Art of Genius

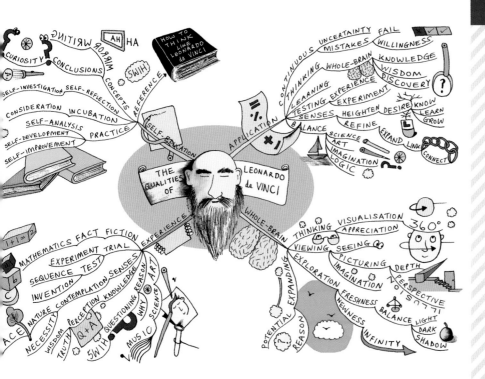

CONTENT
Understanding how
geniuses think

READING SKILL
Paraphrasing

BUILDING VOCABULARY
Understanding adjective
and adverb suffixes

**"Genius is the capacity to see ten things
where the ordinary man sees one."**

— Ezra Pound, American poet and writer (1885–1972)

Before You Read

A. **Connect with the topic.** Identify the profession of each "genius" from the past in the chart below. Then think of someone with a different profession to add to the chart.

Name	Profession	Accomplishments
Galileo		invented the first telescope
Mozart		composed more than 600 pieces of music
Dickens		wrote many famous novels

B. **Pair work.** Compare charts with your partner. Based on this information, how would you define the word "genius"?

C. **Preview the reading.** Look quickly over the reading on pages 133–135 to complete the Previewing Chart below.

> ## Previewing Chart
>
> 1. Title of the reading: _____
>
> 2. Names of people in the reading. (List 3 more.)
>
>   _Darwin_   _____
>
>   _____   _____
>
> 3. Key words. (What words appear several times? List 3 more.)
>
>   _genius_   _____
>
>   _____   _____
>
> 4. Read the first paragraph and the headings. What do you think the reading is probably about?
>
>   _____
>
>   _____
>
>   _____

Reading Passage

The Art of Genius: Six Ways to Think Like Einstein

by Michael Michalko
from *The Futurist/Utne Reader*

1   How do geniuses come up with ideas? What links the thinking
style that produced *Mona Lisa* with the one that spawned[1] the
theory of relativity? What can we learn from the thinking strategies
of the **Galileos**, **Edisons**, and **Mozarts** (*see painting*) of history?

5   For years, scholars tried to study genius by analyzing statistics.
In 1904, Havelock Ellis noted that most geniuses were fathered by
men older than 30, had mothers younger than 25, and usually were
sickly children. Other researchers reported that many were celibate[2]
(Descartes), fatherless (Dickens), or motherless (Darwin). In the
10 end, the data illuminated nothing.

Academics also tried to measure the links between intelligence
and genius. But they found that run-of-the-mill physicists had **IQs**
much higher than **Nobel Prize** winner and extraordinary genius
Richard Feynman, whose IQ was a merely respectable 122. Genius is not
15 about mastering 14 languages at the age of seven or even being especially
smart. Creativity is not the same as intelligence.

Most people of average intelligence can figure out the expected
conventional response to a given problem. For example, when asked, "What
is one-half of 13?" most of us immediately answer six and one-half. That's
20 because we tend to think *reproductively*. When confronted with a problem,
we sift through what we've been taught and what has worked for us in the
past, select the most promising approach, and work toward the solution.

Geniuses, on the other hand, think *productively*. They ask: "How many
different ways can I look at this problem?" and "How many ways can I
25 solve it?" A productive thinker, for example, would find a number of ways
to "halve 13":

6.5
1/3 = 1 and 3
THIR TEEN = 4
30   XI/II = 11 and 2

Culture and
Language Notes
page 157

---

[1] **spawned**   gave birth to; was responsible for
[2] **celibate**   not active sexually

The mark of genius is the willingness to explore *all* the alternatives, not just the most likely solution. Reproductive thinking fosters rigidity.[3] This is why we often fail when we're confronted with a new problem that appears on the surface to be similar to others we've solved, but is,

35 in fact, significantly different. Interpreting a problem through your past experience will inevitably lead you astray.[4] If you think the way you've always thought, you'll get what you've always gotten.

For centuries, the Swiss dominated the watch industry. But in 1968, when a U.S. inventor unveiled[5] a battery-powered watch at the World

40 Watch Congress, every Swiss watch manufacturer rejected it because it didn't fit their limited paradigm.[6] Meanwhile, Seiko, a Japanese electronics company, took one look at the invention and proceeded to change the future of the world watch market.

By studying the notebooks, correspondence, and conversations of

45 some of the world's great thinkers in science, art, and industry, scholars have identified the following thinking strategies that enable geniuses to generate original ideas:

1. Geniuses look at problems from all angles.[7] **Sigmund Freud's** analytical methods were designed to find details that didn't fit

50 traditional paradigms in order to come up with a completely new point of view. To solve a problem creatively, you must abandon the first approach that comes to mind, which usually stems from past experience, and reconceptualize the problem.[8] Geniuses do not merely solve existing problems; they identify new ones.

55 **2. Geniuses make their thought visible.** Geniuses develop visual and spatial abilities that allow them to display information in new ways. The explosion of creativity in the **Renaissance** was tied to the development of graphic illustration during that period, notably the scientific diagrams of **Leonardo da Vinci** and Galileo Galilei. Galileo

60 revolutionized science by making his thought graphically visible while his contemporaries used more conventional means.

3. Geniuses produce. Thomas Edison held 1,093 patents,[9] still a record. He guaranteed a high level of productivity by giving himself idea quotas:[10] one minor invention every ten days and a major invention

---

[3] **fosters rigidity**   leads to uncreative thinking

[4] **lead you astray**   take you in the wrong direction

[5] **unveiled**   showed for the first time

[6] **paradigm**   model that shows how something works

[7] **look at something from all angles**   think about something from many different perspectives

[8] **reconceptualize the problem**   find creative new ways to think about and solve the problem

[9] **held patents**   owned the rights to new inventions

[10] **idea quota**   minimum number of new ideas within a certain time period

65   every six months. Johann Sebastian Bach wrote a cantata[11] every week, even when he was sick or exhausted. Wolfgang Mozart produced more than 600 pieces of music.

4. Geniuses make novel combinations. Like playful children with buckets of building blocks,[12] geniuses constantly combine and
70   recombine ideas, images, and thoughts. The laws of heredity[13] were developed by Gregor Mendel, who combined mathematics and biology to create a new science of genetics.

5. Geniuses force relationships. Their facility[14] to connect the unconnected enables geniuses to see things others miss. Da Vinci
75   noticed the similarity between the sound of a bell and a stone hitting water—and concluded that sound travels in waves.

6. Geniuses prepare themselves for chance. Whenever we attempt to do something and fail, we end up doing something else. That's the first principle of creative accident. We may ask ourselves why we have
80   failed to do what we intended, which is a reasonable question. But the creative accident leads to the question: What have we done? Answering that one in a novel, unexpected way is the essential creative act. It is not luck, but creative insight of the highest order.[15]

This may be the most important lesson of all: When you find something
85   interesting, drop everything and go with it. Too many talented people fail to make significant leaps of imagination because they've become fixated on their pre-conceived plan.[16] But not the truly great minds. They don't wait for gifts of chance; they make them happen.

 Word Count: 874

Reading Time: _____
(Minutes)

Words per Minute: _____
(Word Count/Reading Time)

About the Source

Utne Reader is a bi-monthly magazine that publishes articles from over 2,000 sources. Subtitled "The Best of the Alternative Media," *Utne Reader* covers topics including race, feminism, environment, global politics, art, media, humor, relationships, and in-depth news.

---

11 **cantata**   piece of religious music with singing
12 **building blocks**   small pieces of wood that children play with
13 **heredity**   scientific process of passing qualities from parents to children
14 **facility**   ability to do something well
15 **highest order**   highest level or quality
16 **become fixated on their pre-conceived plan**   are only able to think about their original plan

After You Read

Understanding the Text

A. Comprehension
For each item below, fill in the correct circle.

1. **Finding the Main Idea** The main idea of the reading is:
   - (A) Geniuses are different from other people because they work hard.
   - (B) Geniuses are different from other people because they think productively.
   - (C) The most intelligent people are not necessarily geniuses.
   - (D) There aren't many geniuses in the world.

2. **Scanning for Details** According to paragraph 3, which of the following statements is true about Richard Feynman?
   - (A) He had an unusually high IQ.
   - (B) He could speak many languages.
   - (C) He did not have an unusually high IQ.
   - (D) He was not highly creative.

3. **Using Context** The word *illuminated* in line 10 is closest in meaning to ____.
   - (A) showed
   - (B) helped
   - (C) made sick
   - (D) designed

4. **Using Context** The word *mastering* in line 15 is closest in meaning to ____.
   - (A) teaching
   - (B) finding
   - (C) learning
   - (D) solving

5. **Making Inferences** It may be concluded that the author thinks that Galileo was a genius because ____.
   - (A) he was very intelligent
   - (B) he worked hard
   - (C) he was a creative thinker
   - (D) he mastered many languages

B. Consider the Issues
Work with a partner to answer the questions below.

1. How are geniuses different from the rest of the population? What special abilities or skills do geniuses have that other people don't have?

2. The author outlines six "thinking strategies" that help geniuses develop original ideas. In your opinion, which of these strategies is most important to the success of a scientist? An artist? A businessperson? Why?

Building Vocabulary

Understanding Adjective and Adverb Suffixes

Many adjectives in English are formed by adding a suffix at the end of a verb or noun. The most common suffixes are *–al*, *-ent*, *-ive*, *-ous*, *-ful*, and *-less*.

Example: *father* (noun) + *-less* (suffix) = *fatherless* (adjective)

Many adverbs in English are formed by adding the suffix *–ly* at the end of adjectives.

Example: *productive* (adjective) + *-ly* (suffix) = *productively* (adverb)

You can easily expand your vocabulary by learning the different forms of a word. You can keep track of the words you learn in a word form chart like the one in Activity A below.

A. Scan the reading on pages 133–135 to find either the adjective or adverb form of each word in the chart below. Then use what you know about suffixes to write the other form of the word.

Noun	Verb	Adjective	Adverb
1. tradition			
2. significance	signify		
3. productivity	produce		
4. play	play		
5. vision	envision		
6. convention			
7. origin	originate		
8. creativity	create		
9. space	space		
10. difference	differ		

B. Now use a word from the chart to complete each sentence below. (More than one answer may be possible.)

1. The birth of a child is a _____ event in the development of a family.

2. Geniuses are more _____ than ordinary people.

3. Artists usually have very good _____ memories. They can remember clearly what they saw.

4. A suit and tie is _____ office attire for a male professional in the United States.

5. I live in England now, but I'm _____ from Turkey.

Reading Skill

Paraphrasing

Paraphrasing means saying the same thing with different words. Paraphrasing helps you to understand and remember what you have read.

When you paraphrase a sentence, you use different words and different grammatical structures, but you don't change the meaning of the original sentence.

  Original sentence: Creativity is not the same as intelligence.
✓Good paraphrase: Being creative and being intelligent are different things.
✗Bad paraphrase: Creativity is different from intelligence. (*too similar*)
✗Bad paraphrase: It's difficult to be intelligent and creative.
                      (*different meaning*)

A. Analyze the Reading

Ask yourself the questions in the box to evaluate each set of paraphrases below. Then choose the best paraphrase in each group.

Is it different enough from the original?	Does it contain the same information?

1. Original: For years, scholars tried to study geniuses by analyzing statistics.

    Paraphrase: **a.** To learn about geniuses, researchers spent years looking at statistics.

                       b. Scholars attempted to study geniuses for years by analyzing statistics.

                       c. Researchers have spent a lot of time analyzing geniuses.

2. Original: The mark of a genius is the willingness to explore *all* the alternatives, not just the most likely solution.

    Paraphrase: **a.** The sign of a genius is the willingness to look into all the alternatives, not just the most likely solution.

                       b. A genius is someone who is willing to ignore the most likely solution.

                       c. Geniuses don't look for the most obvious solution to a problem; they want to look at all the possible solutions.

3. Original: To solve a problem creatively, you must abandon the first approach that comes to mind.

    Paraphrase: **a.** If you want to be a creative problem solver, you can't always go with your first idea.

                       b. You must abandon the first idea that comes to mind to solve a problem creatively.

                       c. If you want to approach an idea creatively, you must abandon it.

B. Apply the Reading Skill

Choose one of the facts about Einstein below and paraphrase it. Then ask your classmates to evaluate your paraphrase.

Five Fascinating Facts About Albert Einstein

As a child, Albert Einstein was slow to speak. Even at the age of six, he did not speak well. He thought for a long time before answering a question, and his parents were afraid he was abnormal.

Einstein hated the strict discipline of school and certain subjects that required memorization. When asked what work the boy should pursue, a class teacher said it did not matter; he would never make a success of anything.

Thinking back on his childhood, Einstein felt that his backwardness actually helped him. A "normal" adult does not stop to think about space and time, he said, because he has already done so as a child. In his case, because he wondered about the universe after he was grown, he went into it more deeply.

He tried to make life as simple as possible so that he would have more time for his work. He wore his hair long in later years so he world not have to go to the barber, and he felt socks were unnecessary.

Einstein died at the age of 76. He did not want a funeral, grave, or monument. He also did not want his house turned into a museum, and he wanted his office used by others. He left his brain to research, but doctors found nothing unusual in its size, weight, or formation.

My paraphrase:

_____

_____

_____

_____

Discussion & Writing

1. Who are the geniuses of our time? Think of a modern-day genius and add notes to the chart below.

Name	Profession	Why a genius?
Oktay Sinanoğlu	scientist	very productive
		combines ideas in different ways
		experiments with different sciences

2. Write a paragraph describing the person you chose. Explain why you think this person is a genius.

Example

Some people call Oktay Sinanoğlu "The Turkish Einstein." He is Turkey's most famous scientist and the winner of many international awards for his contributions to science. Like most geniuses, Sinanoğlu has a high level of productivity. He completed his Ph.D. in only two years and became a full professor at Yale University at the age of 26! Sinanoğlu also has a genius's ability to put ideas into new combinations. For example, although he specializes in chemistry and molecular biology, his research also draws from mathematics. Additionally, Sinanoğlu has worked for improvements in education and for the preservation of the Turkish language and culture.

Mini-Dictionary
page 163

Words to Remember

NOUNS	VERBS	ADJECTIVES
alternative	abandon	essential
image	analyze	extraordinary
link	confront	significant
method	dominate	
view	enable	
	generate	
	intend	
	note	
	proceed	
	tend	

Benefits *Benefits* (or *employee benefits*) are ways of compensating employees in addition to their regular earnings. Some examples of benefits are health insurance, retirement savings plans, childcare, money for education, vacation days, and sick days.

Revenue *Revenue* (also called *gross income*) is the total amount of money an organization earns during a specific period of time, for the goods it sells or the services it provides. From this amount, business costs are subtracted to determine the *net income*.

Attorney In the United States, the terms *attorney* and *lawyer* are used interchangeably. An attorney is someone who has attended law school, passed an exam, and practices law. Some attorneys and lawyers work in court (bringing cases to trial), and some do not. A corporate attorney might write legal documents or advise the company on business proposals. In some other countries (Canada, the UK, and Australia, for example), there are two types of attorneys called *barristers* and *solicitors*.

Vice president of corporate communications A *vice president* is the second-highest ranking person in an American organization, following the president. Within an organization, *corporate communications* is a department that shares the company's news, practices, or goals with the public. Another term for this department is *public relations*.

Chapter 2 | Culture and Language Notes

Africa Separated from Europe by the Mediterranean Sea, *Africa* is the second largest continent with the second highest population (one billion people). Almost 15% of the world's population lives in Africa. Anthropologists consider Africa to be the oldest inhabited place and have found signs of humans living there seven million years ago. There are 54 countries in Africa, and over 2,000 languages are spoken. The most visited places in Africa are Egypt and South Africa.

Soccer *Soccer* is a sport in which two teams try to kick a ball into a goal at the opposing team's end of a field. The sport is known to most countries as *football*, but it is called *soccer* in the United States and Canada. (*American football* is a sport involving a different type of ball and more ways of moving the ball toward a goal.) Soccer is a very old sport, dating back to the ancient Greeks and Romans. Today it is extremely popular worldwide, especially in South America and Africa. The biggest international soccer competition is the World Cup, which takes place every four years.

Philippines A chain of 7,107 islands makes up the southeastern Asian country of the *Philippines*. Many of the islands are mountainous and covered with tropical rainforest. A population of 92 million people makes the Philippines the twelfth most populous country in the world. In addition, 11 million Filipinos (people from the Philippines) live in other parts of the world. The Philippines were first controlled by Spain (in the 1500s) and later by the United States. The Philippines became an independent country after World War II, but English, along with Filipino, are the official languages today.

Indonesia Located near the Philippines in Southeast Asia, *Indonesia* is an island country. It is made up of 17,508 islands, of which 6,000 are inhabited. The biggest, most well-known islands are Java, Sumatra, Borneo, and New Guinea. With a population of 238 million, Indonesia is the world's fourth most populous country. It is also a diverse country, with thousands of regional languages and 300 ethnic groups. The landscape of Indonesia has many natural resources, including beaches and jungles, which have drawn international tourists to the region (especially to the island of Bali). It also has 150 active volcanoes and experiences frequent earthquakes.

World Economic Forum The *World Economic Forum*, based in Switzerland, is an international organization that promotes new business ideas to help the world. Its members believe that economic progress and social development go together. The organization also encourages world leaders to become more involved in local communities. The Young Global Leaders Forum chooses 100-200 young leaders from all over the world every year to share their ideas at conferences and other events. The biggest annual conference is held in Davos, Switzerland.

Chapter 3 | Culture and Language Notes

Harvard University *Harvard University* is the oldest and most famous university in North America. Founded in 1636, Harvard is a private university located in Cambridge, Massachusetts, near Boston. There are about 18,000 undergraduate and graduate students at Harvard and 2,000 faculty members. Barack Obama, John F. Kennedy, and six other United States presidents were Harvard University graduates, and more than 40 members of its faculty have been Nobel Prize winners.

Senior *Seniors* are students in their final year of high school or college. First-year students are called *freshmen*; second-year students are *sophomores*; and students in their third year of high school or college are *juniors*.

Learning team A *learning team*, also called a *study group*, is a group of students that meets on a regular basis to talk about class readings, study for exams, and do other things to improve the students' grades.

Highlighting and margin notes *Highlighting* and *taking margin notes* are two ways to help you record and remember important information when you read. You highlight by using a colored pen to mark the important words, sentences, or paragraphs that you want to remember and review later. You write margin notes next to important ideas in the book you are reading. (The margin is the white space around the edges of the page.) Your margin notes could be of various types:

- General reactions to the reading (e.g., *Great idea!*)
- Connections between the reading and your own life (e.g., *This city sounds like the place where I grew up.*)
- Questions about the reading (e.g., *What is the main idea here?*)

Office hours Most professors in American universities hold *office hours* every week to help students with any questions they have. Professors usually set aside three to four hours at the same time each week for their office hours. Students usually do not need to make an appointment to visit their professors during office hours. It is a time for a professor and a student to have a more casual conversation and for the professor to give help and advice.

National survey A *national survey* is used to find out public opinion on a particular issue. There are many professional groups and companies that take national surveys. They ask hundreds or thousands of people the same set of questions and then report the results. Many businesses use national surveys to see how popular or effective their products are. During election campaigns, national surveys are often used to show how popular the different candidates are or how the voters feel about specific political issues.

Learning disabilities Some students have *learning disabilities*, or problems with learning, which make it hard for the brain to receive, process, analyze, or store information. Learning disabilities can affect people's ability to concentrate (to focus attention on something), read, write, speak, understand visual information, or do math. Learning disabilities are not the same as *learning styles*, which describe the ways in which people learn most effectively, e.g., through seeing, through listening, etc. Learning disabilities do not go away, but after a disability is diagnosed, students can work with a special tutor or teacher, or use special equipment, to improve their ability to learn. Learning disabilities do not affect a person's intelligence; many geniuses, such as Albert Einstein, have had learning disabilities.

Institute for Learning and Brain Sciences Located at the University of Washington in Seattle, Washington, the *Institute for Learning and Brain Sciences* studies how humans learn. Its members conduct research on learning and development at all stages of life. Researchers come from various academic disciplines (fields of study), such as psychology, biology, linguistics, education, and neuroscience. They communicate their research results to people all over the world who are interested in the science of learning.

Electrical language pathways *Electrical language pathways* in the brain are also called *neural pathways*, or *nerves* (which run by electricity). These nerves control how the brain processes language.

Chapter 5 | Culture and Language Notes

Rorschach test In 1921, a German psychologist named Hermann Rorschach created a psychological test based on ten images of inkblots (ink patterns on paper). The test is also known as the *Rorschach Inkblot Test* or the *Inkblot Test*. The ten inkblots appear to have no meaning. However, Rorschach believed that a person's interpretations of the shapes, and how they answered questions about them, could give information about a person's personality and emotions. The test was the most popular psychological test used in the 1960s. The test is still sometimes used today, though critics think it is not valid or reliable, especially since the inkblot images are widely available for viewing.

Aztecs The *Aztecs* were made up of several ethnic groups of people who lived in central Mexico in the 14th, 15th, and 16th centuries. The first Aztecs built a big and powerful city in what is now known as Mexico City. They gradually conquered (took over) surrounding areas and expanded their empire so that it covered much of Central Mexico. During the time of Spanish colonization of the Americas, the Spanish conqueror Hernán Cortés led an attack on the Aztecs. The Aztec Empire fell in 1521 when the last Aztec emperor surrendered to Hernán Cortés. The Spanish rebuilt the capital city and renamed it Mexico City.

Indra *Indra* is a character in Hindu mythology. He is the king of the gods, a great warrior, defending both gods and humans against evil. He is also known as the god of war and the god of weather (specifically, of storms, rain, and thunder). In art, he is commonly shown as a thunder god, carrying a lightning bolt as a weapon.

Heng O *Heng O* (or *Heng-O*) is the Chinese goddess of the moon. According to legend, she tried to steal from her husband a drink that would make her live forever and let her rise up to Heaven. Her husband caught her drinking it and stopped her before she finished. Since she only finished half of the drink, she could not rise as far as she wanted to and instead settled on the moon.

Plutarch (c. 46–120 CE) *Plutarch* was a historian, biographer, and essay writer who was born in Greece and later became a Roman citizen. He is famous for writing *The Lives of the Roman Emperors from Augustus to Vitellius* and *Parallel Lives*, a series of biographies of famous Greeks and Romans. His writings were a great influence on English and French literature.

Aristarchus (c. 310–230 BCE) *Aristarchus of Samos* was a Greek mathematician and astronomer. He was the first to disagree with Aristotle's idea that the sun moved around the earth, and to suggest instead that the earth moved around the sun. He was also one of the first people to try to calculate the sizes and distances of the sun and the moon.

Chapter 6 | Culture and Language Notes

Culture shock *Culture shock* is the feeling some people experience when they travel to a new country or part of the world for the first time. Sometimes the food, style of dress, and other aspects of life in a new country are so different that people have a hard time adjusting to this new way of life. Culture shock can last for days, weeks, or even months.

Melbourne *Melbourne* is the capital of Victoria, a state in the southeastern part of Australia. There are roughly 3,900,000 people in Melbourne, the second largest city in Australia, after Sydney. Melbourne was established by English settlers in 1835 and is the youngest city of its size in the world. It is a busy trade and manufacturing center that has attracted immigrants from many countries, including Greece, Italy, Poland, Turkey, Cambodia, and Vietnam.

Boston College *Boston College* (BC) is a major American university located just outside Boston in Chestnut Hill, Massachusetts. Founded in 1863, BC is one of the oldest and largest Catholic universities in the United States, with 9,200 undergraduates and 4,000 graduate students. In 2010, there were students from 93 different countries studying at BC.

Exchange students *Exchange students* go to schools or universities outside of their home countries. Each year, more than 1,200,000 students around the world leave their home countries to study abroad. Roughly 670,000 international students come each year to study at colleges or universities in the United States, while about 262,000 Americans study abroad. Many American colleges and universities recruit foreign students to study in their undergraduate and graduate programs.

Boston *Boston* is the capital of the state of Massachusetts, about 200 miles north of New York City on the Atlantic Ocean. About 623,000 people live in the city itself, and about 5,000,000 live in the surrounding suburbs. Boston is one of the oldest and most historically important cities in North America; it was founded in 1630. The Revolutionary War between the American colonies and England began near Boston in 1775. Boston is known for its fine universities, beautiful architecture, and delicious seafood.

Australia *Australia* is the smallest continent on the planet and also one of the largest countries. It is located south of Asia between the Indian and Pacific Oceans. Australia's capital is Canberra, and the largest cities are Sydney, Melbourne, Brisbane, and Perth. The population of Australia is roughly 22,500,000 people, with 91% living in cities. The koala bear, kangaroo, and several other Australian animals are not found in the wild anywhere else in the world.

Massachusetts *Massachusetts* is a state located on the Atlantic Ocean northeast of New York City. It was one of the 13 original American colonies. These colonies got their independence from England in 1783 when they became the United States of America. Roughly half the population of Massachusetts lives in and around the capital city of Boston.

Eating disorders An *eating disorder* is a medical condition relating to food and weight. A person with an eating disorder uses dangerous methods to be thin, including starvation or abuse of diet pills. This behavior can result in serious health problems. Some researchers believe that 64% of American college women show some symptoms of an eating disorder.

Chapter 7 | Culture and Language Notes

Gulf of Mexico The *Gulf of Mexico* is bordered by Mexico to the west and south, Texas and other U.S. states to the north, and the coast of Florida to the east. The ocean water in the Gulf of Mexico is usually calm and warm, but the area is occasionally hit by severe hurricanes.

Super 8 movie Super 8mm film was a popular technology for making home movies in the 1960s and 1970s. These were called *Super 8 movies*. Parents would make movies of their families on vacation, during holidays, and on other special occasions. Videotape technology replaced Super 8 cameras in the 1980s, as video was easier and cheaper to use.

North Carolina *North Carolina* is a U.S. state located in the southeastern part of the country along the Atlantic Ocean. North Carolina borders the states of Virginia, South Carolina, Tennessee, and Georgia. More than 9,250,000 people live in North Carolina, making it the tenth largest state by population in the United States. Raleigh is the capital, and Charlotte is its largest city.

Florida *Florida*, an important U.S. tourist destination, is called *The Sunshine State* and is located in the southeastern corner of the United States. The weather is sunny and warm there for most of the year. There are miles and miles of beaches in Florida along the Atlantic Ocean and the Gulf of Mexico. Tallahassee, situated in the northern part of the state, is the capital, and Miami is its largest city.

Boyfriend In North America, *boyfriend* means a man of any age who has a romantic relationship with someone else. *Girlfriend* is a similar expression that means a woman of any age who has a romantic relationship with someone else. However, a woman may also use the word *girlfriend* to refer to a woman friend.

Sophomore *Sophomores* are students in their second year of high school or college. First-year students are called *freshmen*; third-year students are called *juniors*; and students in their fourth year of high school or college are called *seniors*.

Work part-time Many North American high school and university students *work part-time* while attending school. These students typically work five to 15 hours each week in the afternoons and evenings or on the weekends. A lot of students find part-time work in restaurants and retail stores or as baby-sitters. In general, people must be 14 years old to work legally in the United States, although the legal age varies according to the type of job. The U.S. Department of Labor has guidelines for the maximum number of hours which people under 18 can work.

Straight As American students who get *straight As* usually score between 90 and 100% on all of their tests and receive a grade of "A" in all of their courses. The following chart shows, in general, the different grades given to students in the United States and the corresponding percentages.

Grade	Percentage (%)
A	90–100
B	80–89
C	70–79
D	60–69
F (Fail)	0–59

Braille *Braille* is a system of writing for the blind in which patterns of raised dots represent letters, letter combinations (such as *ch*), some commonly used short words, numbers, and punctuation marks. It can also be used for writing music. Blind people read Braille by running their fingers over rows of the dot patterns. They can write in Braille by making the dot patterns themselves using special equipment.

Turkey *Turkey*, population 75,000,000, is located on the Anatolian peninsula and bridges Europe and Asia. Its European and Asian sections are marked by the Dardanelles, the Sea of Marmara, and the Bosphorus. Because the Anatolian peninsula is one of the oldest inhabited regions in the world, Turkey has a rich cultural heritage. It also has diverse geography: coastline, mountains, plains, and steppes. The greatest tourist attractions are the capital city of Istanbul, the caves and unusual volcanic landscapes of Cappadoccia, and the coast. The Mediterranean coast of Turkey averages 300 sunny days a year.

Ottoman Empire The *Ottoman Empire* began in the early 14th century and lasted for six centuries. At its peak, it ruled the entire eastern Mediterranean region, much of Eastern Europe, and North Africa. The Ottoman Empire was most powerful under the reign of Mehmet the Conqueror (1451–1481) who greatly expanded its rule. Another important leader of the Ottoman Empire was Sultan Suleyman the Magnificent (1520–1566) who made large improvements to Istanbul and extended Ottoman power to Vienna, Austria. The Ottoman Empire declined in the nineteenth century and broke up soon after World War I.

Political rally A large meeting held to support a politician or someone running for public office is called a *political rally*. At political rallies, you often hear loud music and shouting, as these events are designed to excite people about a politician's ideas.

Sermon A *sermon* is a type of speech similar to a lecture. It is usually given by a religious official and at a house of worship or a religious service. A sermon may explain a religious text to an audience, relate a past story to the present time, teach the importance of a religious tradition, or encourage listeners to embrace their religious faith.

Pep rally *Pep rallies* are popular in North American schools. A pep rally is a large meeting before a sports event to show support for the school and the sports team. It is usually noisy, with a lot of yelling, chanting, and music (drums or a marching band).

Mark Twain (1835–1910) *Mark Twain*, one of the U.S.'s most famous authors, is best known for his novels *The Adventures of Tom Sawyer* and *The Adventures of Huckleberry Finn*. These novels have become classics of American literature and are used around the country to teach students in English literature classes.

Tribute to the company treasurer on his/her retirement When an American businessperson leaves his or her job after many years, the company usually throws a *retirement party*. Colleagues typically honor the person by giving toasts, making speeches, and telling stories about the person's contributions to the company.

Edward R. Murrow (1908–1965) *Edward R. Murrow* was one of the greatest American radio and television journalists. He provided Americans with radio news throughout World War II and became famous for his broadcasts from London's rooftops during the German bombing of that city. He was known throughout his life as an excellent public speaker.

Japan Located in northeast Asia, *Japan* is comprised of roughly 3,900 islands with 27,000 kilometers of coastline. The four largest Japanese islands are Kyushu, Shikoku, Hokkaido, and Honshu. With a population of 127 million, Japan is one of the most densely populated countries in the world. Roughly 30 million people live in and around Tokyo, the nation's capital.

Western The term *Western* refers to people, places, or things relating to the *West*, the group of countries including Europe and the United States that share a heritage from Ancient Greece and the Roman Empire. We can, for example, refer to cars manufactured in Sweden, Germany, or the United States as Western cars. A person from the West is sometimes called a *Westerner*. We use the term *Eastern* to talk about Asian people, places, or things.

Volleyball *Volleyball* was invented in the United States in 1895 when William G. Morgan decided to blend the elements of basketball, baseball, tennis, and handball to create an exciting game that would involve minimal physical contact. *Indoor volleyball* became an Olympic sport in 1964 during the Tokyo Olympics, while *beach volleyball* was introduced at Atlanta's Summer Olympic Games in 1996. First made popular on the beaches of California, beach volleyball is now played throughout the world and is especially popular with Brazilians and others living in warm climates.

Bowling Enjoyed in over 90 countries around the world, *bowling* is especially popular in the United States, where 80 million people bowl at least once in a while. Bowling is also extremely popular in Japan. A discovery of objects found in an Egyptian grave seems to suggest that the sport has been around since 3200 BCE.

Chapter 11 | Culture and Language Notes

Letter of application If you are interested in working for an American company, you usually send a *letter of application* and a *résumé* to the company's personnel, or human resources, department. Note that a letter of application is often called a *cover letter*.

Résumé A *résumé* is a short summary of your education and job history. Most résumés are one to three pages long and include only the highlights of your experience.

Help-wanted ad Many people in the United States find their jobs through *help-wanted advertisements* in newspapers or online. Companies are increasingly advertising their job openings on websites. When people are looking for a job, they review the ads and then send a letter of application and résumé to the companies where they would like to work.

Personnel The *personnel department*, also called the *human resources department*, handles the interviewing, hiring, and training of new employees in a company. It is also responsible for handling *benefits* like health insurance and retirement plans. If a company decides that an employee should be fired, the personnel department handles this process.

District attorney A *district attorney* is a lawyer in the United States who works for the government. Many Americans refer to a district attorney as a *D.A.* A district attorney is usually responsible for prosecuting crimes within a particular area.

Reference A *reference* can be two different things. Firstly, a reference can be a *letter* giving information about your skills and personality. This letter is usually written by a former teacher or employer and is often sent to a company for which you would like to work. A reference can also be a *person* whom an employer contacts to ask questions about your background.

Spain *Spain* is the third largest country in Europe and is located in the southwestern corner of the continent. The population of Spain is 46,000,000. Tourism brings 57,000,000 visitors to the country each year. Madrid is the capital, and other important cities include Barcelona, Valencia, Seville, and Granada.

Common Market The official name for the *Common Market* is the *European Union* (EU). The 27 countries in the EU cooperate in a variety of economic and political areas. In 1999, the EU introduced the *euro*, a currency that can be used in most European countries. In 2002, the euro replaced several national currencies.

Countries in the EU are: Austria, Belgium, Bulgaria, Cyprus, the Czech Republic, Denmark, Estonia, Finland, France, Germany, Greece, Hungary, Italy, Latvia, Lithuania, Luxembourg, Malta, the Netherlands, Poland, Portugal, Republic of Ireland, Romania, Slovakia, Slovenia, Spain, Sweden, and the United Kingdom.

Siesta *Siesta* is the Spanish word for a nap, or a short period of sleep in the middle of the day. Many people in Spain and Latin America take a siesta in the afternoon following their lunch. The typical siesta is from 2:00 to 4:30. In the past, almost everyone in Spain took a siesta every day. While this tradition is still popular, fewer people stop for a siesta nowadays. Especially in large cities like Madrid and Barcelona, many professional people work from 9:00 to 5:00 with only a short break for lunch.

Madrid *Madrid*, a city of 3,200,000 people, is the capital of Spain. Located at roughly 600 meters above sea level, Madrid is a city with very hot summers and cool winters. The *Palacio Real*, the enormous royal palace where Spain's king and queen live, is located in the middle of the city.

Standard of living The *standard of living* is a way to describe the quality of living conditions for an individual or of a country. You can measure the standard of living in a country by looking at the average salary, the general quality of housing and health care, the availability of good food, educational opportunities, etc. The adjectives *high* and *low* describe the standard of living in a country or region, e.g., *The standard of living in Sweden is high.*

Frankenstein The creature from the Frankenstein movies is the best-known monster in movie history. Originally, *Frankenstein* was a character in a novel written by Mary Shelley in 1818. This novel, and many of the films based on it, is the story of a "mad scientist" who creates a monster that eventually kills him. The famous Hollywood movie *Frankenstein* (1931) is based on Shelley's novel.

Science fiction *Science fiction* is a kind of fiction that deals with possible future results of new technologies. Science fiction books and movies often focus on people living in space or aliens from other worlds who visit Earth. Famous science fiction writers include Isaac Asimov and Ray Bradbury. The *Star Wars* and *Star Trek* films are some of the most popular and famous science fiction movies of the late 20th century.

Acid rain *Acid rain* is rain that contains a level of acid that is harmful to the environment. It is normal for rainwater to have a certain amount of acid. However, when dangerous chemicals from cars and factories mix with rain, the percentage of acid in the rain can become too high. When this acid rain falls, it can hurt or kill plants and animals.

Greenhouse effect *The greenhouse effect* refers to the way that gases in the atmosphere around the Earth act like the glass ceiling in a greenhouse. Greenhouses are glass buildings that cover flowers and plants so that they can stay warm and grow in the winter. Like a greenhouse, the Earth's atmosphere keeps the heat from the Sun near the Earth so that we stay warm. In recent years, scientists have found that some forms of air pollution in the atmosphere are keeping more heat inside. If greenhouse gases continue to increase, rising temperatures could cause climate changes and result in environmental disasters.

Genetic engineering *Genetic engineering* is an area of science that deals with studying and changing the natural development of plants and animals. By changing the DNA, or genetic structure, of a living thing, scientists can affect the way it grows. For example, they can create new kinds of tomatoes that stay fresh longer. Many people think that this example demonstrates a good use of genetic engineering. However, others feel that modifying living things in this way may not be completely safe in the long term.

Molecular biology *Molecular biology* is an area of science that focuses mainly on cells, the smallest independently-working parts of living things. Molecular biologists are interested in learning about how cells work and interact with each other. Molecular biology also has much in common with other areas of scientific study, such as chemistry and genetics.

East-West tensions After World War II, the communist Soviet Union had control of eastern Europe, while the governments of western Europe and other democracies like the United States and Canada cooperated with each other to stop the spread of communism. This period of *East-West tensions* was called the *Cold War*. During the Cold War, countries on both sides built nuclear weapons and developed strong armies in case they had to go to war. In the late 1980s, however, many countries in eastern Europe began to reject Soviet control. By 1995, there were democracies throughout eastern Europe and the former Soviet Union. During the 1990s, East-West tensions were greatly reduced.

Chapter 14 | Culture and Language Notes

Mona Lisa The *Mona Lisa* is probably the most famous painting in Western art. It was painted by Leonardo da Vinci in 1504. Thousands of people see the *Mona Lisa* every day in the Louvre Museum in Paris. The *Mona Lisa* is a small picture of a wealthy woman from Florence, Italy, who seems to be smiling very slightly. For 500 years, people have talked about what this mysterious smile means.

Theory of relativity Albert Einstein (1879–1955) is one of the greatest scientists the world has ever known. His general *theory of relativity* explains his theory of gravity, as well as more general scientific concepts. (*Gravity* refers to the force which causes objects to fall toward Earth.) Published in 1915, Einstein's theory of relativity is a general framework that allows us to understand the birth of our universe, its current structure, and ideas about the future development of the solar system.

Galileo Galilei (1564–1642) *Galileo* was a famous Italian astronomer and mathematician. After developing the first telescope, Galileo spent much of his time observing and writing about the stars and planets. He was the first to discover, for example, the moons around the planet Jupiter.

Thomas Alva Edison (1847–1931) The American inventor *Thomas Alva Edison* is responsible for a large number of inventions that have changed our world. He is best known for inventing the light bulb and the record player, but these are only two of his more than 1,000 inventions. Edison also developed the carbon transmitter that allowed Alexander Graham Bell to invent the telephone.

Wolfgang Amadeus Mozart (1756–1791) The Austrian musician *Wolfgang Amadeus Mozart* was one of the greatest composers of classical music. Mozart was an amazing child who could play and write great music by the age of six. During his short life, Mozart composed more than 600 pieces of music. These include the operas *The Marriage of Figaro* and *Don Giovanni* as well as 41 symphonies and many concertos. *Amadeus* is a popular American film about the composer's life.

IQ An *IQ* is used to measure a person's level of intelligence. The letters *IQ* stand for *intelligence quotient*. IQ tests measure certain mental abilities that have been traditionally associated with intelligence. On an IQ test, the average score is 100. Many people argue that an IQ test is not a good way to measure a person's intelligence because it only tests a few abilities. In the past few years, educational researchers have argued that we should look at many factors when measuring a person's intelligence, such as the ability to get along with others, athletic skills, or musical ability.

Nobel Prize Six *Nobel Prizes* are given each year to people who have made the most important contributions in the fields of physics, chemistry, medicine, economics, and literature, as well as to the person or people who have done the most to promote peace in the world. The Nobel Prizes were established by the Swedish inventor Alfred Bernhard Nobel and were first given in 1901. Receiving a Nobel Prize is considered by many to be one of the greatest honors in the world.

Richard Feynman (1918–1988) *Richard Feynman* was an American physicist from New York who is most famous for his work on the Manhattan Project from 1941 to 1945. On this top-secret project, Feynman and a group of other scientists worked to develop the first atomic bombs. Twenty years later, Feynman won the 1965 Nobel Prize in physics for his work in a field called *quantum electrodynamics*.

Sigmund Freud (1856–1939) *Sigmund Freud* is the father of psychoanalysis and the most important person in the history of psychology. Psychoanalysis is a medical method of curing mental illness. Freud was an Austrian doctor who began experimenting in the 1890s with a "talking cure" to assist his patients who were mentally ill. In 1900, Freud published his most important book, *The Interpretation of Dreams*. Throughout his career, Freud argued that thinking and talking about your dreams was an important way to achieve mental health.

Renaissance *Renaissance* is a French word that means *rebirth*. We use this term to refer to the period in Europe between roughly 1400 and 1550. For more than 1000 years, the writings and the art of the Greeks and Romans had been forgotten by Europeans. The Renaissance was a time of "rebirth" because of a new interest in classical Greek and Roman art and ideas. Great masterpieces like da Vinci's *Mona Lisa* and Michelangelo's statue *David* were completed during the *High Renaissance*, the final years of this period in history.

Leonardo da Vinci (1452 –1519) *Leonardo da Vinci* was a remarkable man; an exceptional painter, architect, sculptor, and engineer, he was perhaps the greatest genius of the Italian Renaissance. His most famous painting is the *Mona Lisa*. Da Vinci's notebooks show his amazing understanding of the human body, as well as his creative ideas for many inventions that we have today, including the contact lens and the airplane.

Map 1 Europe

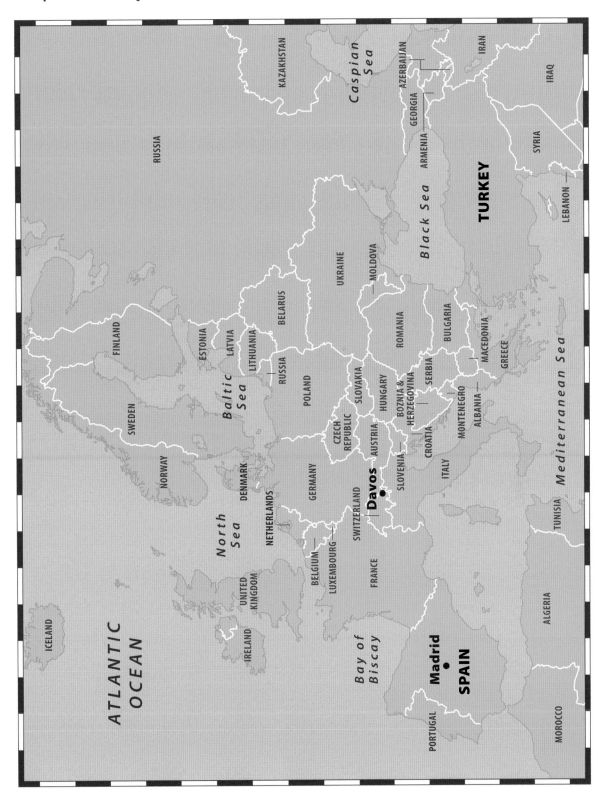

Map 2 South Pacific

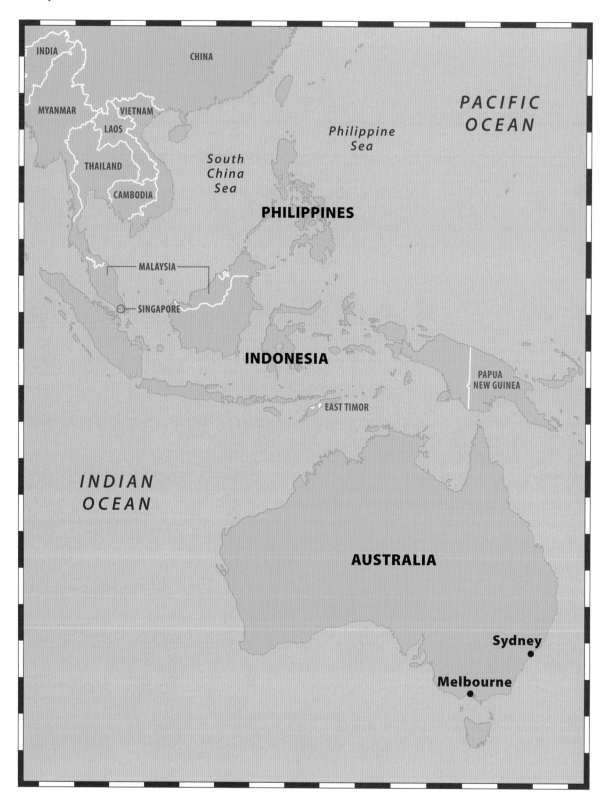

INDIA

CHINA

MYANMAR

VIETNAM

LAOS

THAILAND

CAMBODIA

South
China
Sea

*Philippine
Sea*

**PACIFIC
OCEAN**

MALAYSIA

SINGAPORE

PHILIPPINES

INDONESIA

PAPUA
NEW GUINEA

EAST TIMOR

*INDIAN
OCEAN*

AUSTRALIA

Sydney

Melbourne

Map 3 Eastern United States

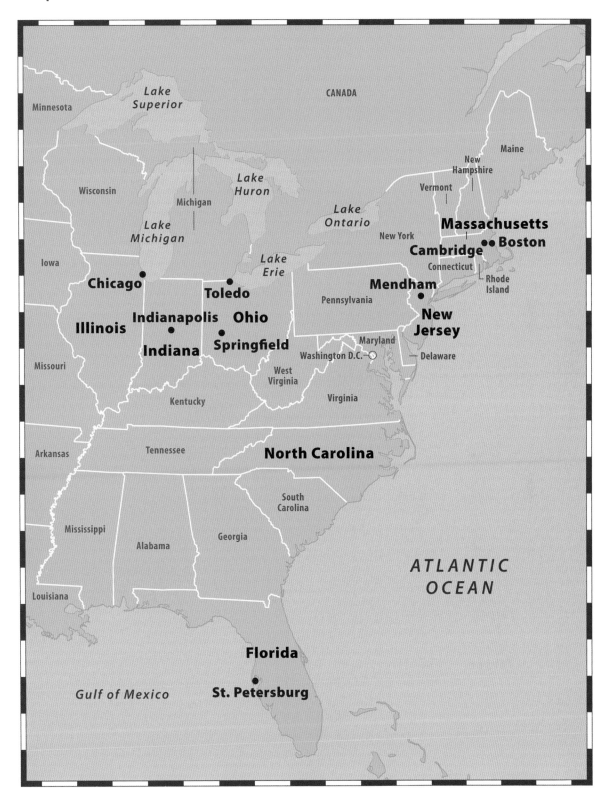

Minnesota

Lake Superior

CANADA

Wisconsin

Lake Huron

Michigan

Maine

New Hampshire

Vermont

Lake Ontario

Lake Michigan

Iowa

New York

Massachusetts

Cambridge

Boston

Lake Erie

Connecticut

Rhode Island

Chicago

Toledo

Mendham

Pennsylvania

Illinois

Indianapolis

Ohio

New Jersey

Indiana

Springfield

Maryland

Missouri

Washington D.C.

Delaware

West Virginia

Virginia

Kentucky

Arkansas

Tennessee

North Carolina

South Carolina

Mississippi

Georgia

Alabama

ATLANTIC OCEAN

Louisiana

Florida

Gulf of Mexico

St. Petersburg

Map 4   East Asia

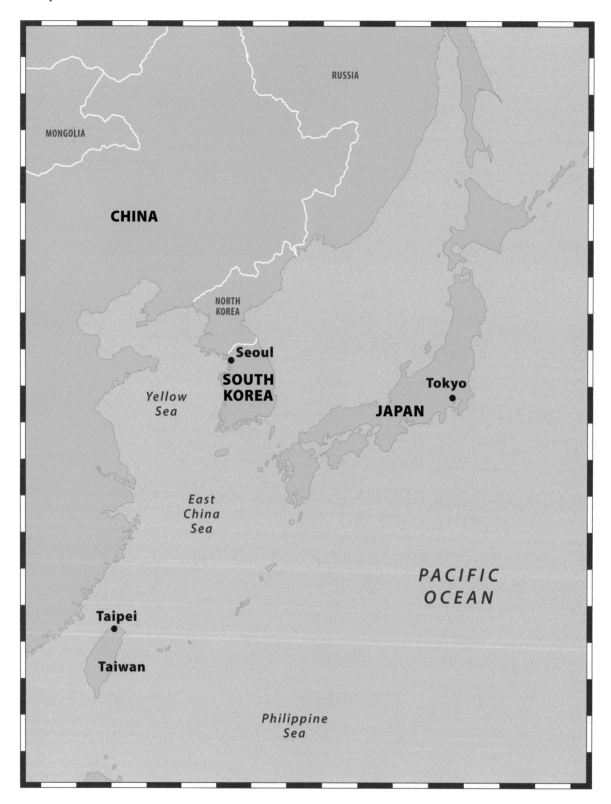

Mini-Dictionary

All dictionary content is taken from the *Oxford American Dictionary for learners of English* © Oxford University Press. All words in the Mini-Dictionary are from the Oxford 3000™ word list. The Oxford 3000™ are the words that are used most often across the widest range of contexts, so they are important words to know, and to know well.

AWL Academic Word List
The Academic Word List contains 570 words that are commonly used in academic English.

a·ban·don **AWL** /əˈbændən/ *verb* to stop doing something without finishing it or without achieving what you wanted to do: *The search for the missing sailors was abandoned after two days.*

a·bil·i·ty /əˈbɪləti/ *noun* the mental or physical power or skill that makes it possible to do something: *A person of his ability will have no difficulty getting a job.*

a·buse /əˈbyuz/ *verb* to treat someone badly, often violently: *The victim had been sexually abused.*

ac·cu·rate **AWL** /ˈækyərət/ *adj.* careful and exact; without mistakes: *an accurate description of the house*

a·chieve·ment **AWL** /əˈtʃivmənt/ *noun* something that is done successfully, especially through hard work or skill: *She considered the book her greatest achievement.*

ac·tion /ˈækʃn/ *verb*
take action to do something in order to solve a problem, etc.: *The governor promised to take action to reduce unemployment in the state.*

ac·tu·al /ˈæktʃuəl/ *adj.* real; that happened: *The actual damage to the car was not as great as we had thought it might be.*

a·dapt **AWL** /əˈdæpt/ *verb* to change something so that you can use it in a different situation: *The van was adapted for use by a person in a wheelchair.*

ad·just **AWL** /əˈdʒʌst/ *verb* to get used to new conditions or a new situation: *She found it hard to adjust to working at night.*

ad·van·tage /ədˈvæntɪdʒ/ *noun* something that may help you to do better than other people: *Her management experience gave her an advantage over other job candidates.*

ag·gres·sive /əˈɡrɛsɪv/ *adj.* using or showing force or pressure in order to succeed: *an aggressive salesman*

al·ter·na·tive **AWL** /ɔlˈtərnətɪv/ *noun* one of two or more things that you can choose between: *There are several alternatives available to us right now.*

am·bi·tion /æmˈbɪʃn/ *noun* a strong desire to be successful, to have power, etc.: *One problem with young people today is their lack of ambition.*

an·a·lyze **AWL** /ˈænəlaɪz/ *verb* to look at or think about the different parts or details of something carefully in order to understand or explain it: *The water samples are now being analyzed in a laboratory.*

an·tic·i·pate **AWL** /ænˈtɪsəpeɪt/ *verb* to expect something to happen (and to prepare for it): *I anticipate that the situation will get worse.*

anx·i·e·ty /æŋˈzaɪəti/ *noun* a feeling of worry or fear, especially about the future: *There are anxieties over the effects of unemployment.*

ap·pre·ci·ate **AWL** /əˈpriʃieɪt/ *verb* to enjoy something or to understand the value of someone or something: *My boss doesn't appreciate me.*

ap·proach **AWL** /əˈproʊtʃ/ *noun* a way of dealing with someone or something: *Parents don't always know what approach to take with teenagers.*

ap·pro·pri·ate **AWL** /əˈproʊpriət/ *adj.* suitable or right for a particular situation, person, use, etc.: *I don't think this movie is appropriate for children.*

ar·gu·ment /ˈɑrɡyumənt/ *noun* the reason(s) that you give to support your opinion about something: *His argument was that if they bought a smaller car, they would save money.*

as·pect `AWL` /ˈæspɛkt/ *noun* one of the qualities or parts of a situation, idea, problem, etc.: *This is the most important aspect of the debate.*

as·sume `AWL` /əˈsum/ *verb* to accept or believe that something is true even though you have no proof; to expect something to be true: *I assume that you have the necessary documents.*

as·sure `AWL` /əˈʃʊr/ *verb* to promise someone that something will certainly happen or be true, especially if he/she is worried: *I assure you that it is perfectly safe.*

at·ten·tion /əˈtɛnʃn/ *noun* the act of watching, listening to, or thinking about something carefully: *Can you get the waiter's attention?*

at·ti·tude `AWL` /ˈæṭətud/ *noun* the way that you think, feel, or behave: *She has a very positive attitude toward her work.*

au·di·ence /ˈɔdiəns/ *noun* the group of people who are watching or listening to a play, concert, speech, the television, etc.: *The audience was wild with excitement.*

au·thor·i·ty `AWL` /əˈθɔrəṭi; əˈθɑr-/ *noun* a person with special knowledge: *She's an authority on ancient Egypt.*

a·vail·a·ble `AWL` /əˈveɪləbl/ *adj.* (used about things) that you can get, buy, use, etc.: *Are there still tickets available for the concert?*

av·er·age /ˈævrɪdʒ/ *adj.* normal or typical: *children of above/below average intelligence*

a·void /əˈvɔɪd/ *verb* to prevent something from happening or to try not to do something: *He always tried to avoid an argument if possible.*

a·ware `AWL` /əˈwɛr/ *adj.* knowing about or realizing something; conscious of someone or something: *I am aware of the difficulties you face.*

back·ground /ˈbækgraʊnd/ *noun* facts or events that are connected with a situation: *The talks are taking place against a background of increasing tension.*

ba·sic /ˈbeɪsɪk/ *adj.* forming the part of something that is most necessary and from which other things develop: *The basic question is, can we afford it?*

ba·sis /ˈbeɪsəs/ *noun* the principle or reason that lies behind something: *We made our decision on the basis of your reports.*

bit·ter /ˈbɪṭər/ *adj.* (used about a person) very unhappy or angry about something that has happened; disappointed: *She was very bitter about the way the company treated her.*

brief `AWL` /brif/ *adj.* short or quick: *Please be brief. We don't have much time.*

bright /braɪt/ *adj.* having a lot of light: *a bright, sunny day*

cap·i·tal /ˈkæpəṭl/ *noun* an amount of money that you use to start a business or to invest so that you earn more money on it: *When she had enough capital, she bought some new equipment.*

chal·lenge `AWL` /ˈtʃæləndʒ/ *noun* something new and difficult that forces you to make a lot of effort: *After over 15 years at her old job, Laura wanted a new challenge.*

char·ac·ter·is·tic /ˌkærəktəˈrɪstɪk/ *noun* a quality that is typical of someone or something and that makes him/her/it different from other people or things: *The chief characteristic of reptiles is that they are cold-blooded.*

charge /tʃɑrdʒ/ *verb* to put electricity into something: *to charge a battery*

com·mand /kəˈmænd/ *noun* control over someone or something: *General Weston has numerous advisers under his command.*

com·pe·ti·tion /ˌkɑmpəˈtɪʃn/ *noun* a situation where two or more people are trying to achieve the same thing or gain an advantage: *There was fierce competition among the players for places on the team.*

com·plete /kəmˈplit/ *adj.* (only before a noun) as great as is possible; in every way: *It was a complete waste of time.*

com·pli·cat·ed /ˈkɑmpləkeɪṭəd/ *adj.* difficult to understand; made up of many parts: *I can't tell you all the details now— it's too complicated.*

con·cen·tra·tion `AWL` /ˌkɑnsnˈtreɪʃn/ *noun* the act of giving all your attention or effort to something: *This type of work requires total concentration.*

con·cept AWL /ˈkɑnsɛpt/ *noun* an idea; a basic principle: *The basic concepts of physics can be difficult to understand.*

con·di·tion /kənˈdɪʃn/ *noun* an illness: *to have a heart condition*

con·fi·dence /ˈkɑnfədəns/ *noun* the feeling that you are sure about your own abilities, opinion, etc.: *"Of course we will win," the coach said with confidence.*

con·front /kənˈfrʌnt/ *verb* to think about, or to make someone think about, something that is difficult or unpleasant: *When the police confronted him with the evidence, he confessed.*

con·nec·tion /kəˈnɛkʃn/ *noun* an association or a relationship between two or more people or things: *There is a clear connection between crime and drug addiction.*

con·si·der /kənˈsɪdər/ *verb* to think about someone or something, often before making a decision: *We must consider the matter carefully before we make our choice.*

con·tact AWL /ˈkɑntækt/ *noun* meeting, talking to, or writing to someone else: *We are in close contact with our office in Ontario.*

con·tain /kənˈteɪn/ *verb* to have something inside or as part of itself: *Each box contains 24 cans.*

con·tri·bu·tion AWL /ˌkɑntrəˈbyuʃn/ *noun* something that you give or do together with others; the act of giving your share: *He made a significant contribution to the country's struggle for independence.*

con·ven·tion·al AWL /kənˈvɛnʃənl/ *adj.* following what is traditional or considered to be normal: *The house was built with conventional materials but in a totally new style.*

cre·ate AWL /kriˈeɪt/ *verb* to cause something new to happen or exist: *a plan to create new jobs in the area*

crit·i·cal /ˈkrɪtɪkl/ *adj.* very important; at a time when things can suddenly become better or worse: *The talks between the two leaders have reached a critical stage.*

cru·cial AWL /ˈkruʃl/ *adj.* extremely important: *Early diagnosis of the illness is crucial for successful treatment.*

cure /kyʊr/ *noun* a medicine or treatment that can cure an illness, etc.: *There is no known cure for AIDS.*

deal /dil/ *verb*
deal with to treat someone a particular way; to handle someone: *He's a difficult man. No one really knows how to deal with him.*

de·bate /dɪˈbeɪt/ *verb* to discuss something in a formal way or at a public debate: *Politicians will be debating the bill later this week.*

dem·on·strate AWL /ˈdɛmənstreɪt/ *verb* to show clearly that something exists or is true; to prove something: *The prison escape demonstrates the need for greater security.*

de·pend /dɪˈpɛnd/ *verb*
depend on to be sure that someone or something will help you; to trust someone or something to do something: *If you ever need any help, you know you can depend on me.*

de·serve /dɪˈzərv/ *verb* to earn something, either good or bad, because of something that you have done: *We've done a lot of work and we deserve a break.*

de·stroy /dɪˈstrɔɪ/ *verb* to damage something so badly that you cannot use it anymore or it does not exist anymore: *The building was destroyed by fire.*

de·ter·mine /dɪˈtərmən/ *verb* to decide or calculate something: *The results of the tests will determine what treatment you need.*

de·vel·op·ment /dɪˈvɛləpmənt/ *noun* a new event: *a number of new developments in the situation in the Middle East*

de·vice AWL /dɪˈvaɪs/ *noun* a tool or piece of equipment made for a particular purpose: *a security device that detects movement*

di·a·gram /ˈdaɪəgræm/ *noun* a simple picture that is used to explain how something works or what something looks like: *a diagram of the body's digestive system*

dif·fer·ence /ˈdɪfrəns/ *noun*
make a, some, etc. difference to have an effect on someone or something: *A week of vacation made a big difference to her health.*

dif·fi·cul·ty /ˈdɪfɪkəlti/ *noun* a situation that is hard to deal with: *We didn't have any difficulty selling our car.*

dis·cov·er /dɪsˈkʌvər/ *verb* to find or learn something new or unexpected, or something that you did not know before: *I think I discovered why the computer won't print out.*

dis·tin·guish /dɪsˈtɪŋgwɪʃ/ *verb* to recognize the difference between things or people: *People who are color blind often can't distinguish red from green.*

dom·i·nate AWL /ˈdɑməneɪt/ *verb* to be more powerful, important, or noticeable than others: *The Raiders' offense dominated throughout the second half of the game.*

edge /ɛdʒ/ *noun* the place where something, especially a surface, ends: *the edge of a table*

ef·fec·tive /ɪˈfɛktɪv/ *adj.* producing the result that you want: *Scientists are looking for an effective way to reduce energy consumption.*

e·merge AWL /ɪˈmərdʒ/ *verb* to appear or come out from somewhere: *A man emerged from the shadows.*

em·pha·sis AWL /ˈɛmfəsəs/ *noun* (giving) special importance or attention (to something): *There's a lot of emphasis on science at our school.*

em·pha·size AWL /ˈɛmfəsaɪz/ *verb* to place importance on something: *They emphasized that healthy eating is important.*

en·a·ble AWL /ɛˈneɪbl/ *verb* to make it possible for someone or something to do something: *Computer technology enables us to predict the weather more accurately.*

en·cour·age·ment /ɪnˈkərɪdʒmənt/ *noun* the act of encouraging someone to do something; something that encourages someone: *He needs all the encouragement he can get.*

end /ɛnd/ *verb*
end up to find yourself in a place/ situation that you did not intend or expect: *We got lost and ended up in a bad part of town.*

en·sure AWL /ɪnˈʃʊr/ *verb* to make something certain to happen: *a plan that would ensure a victory in the election*

en·ter·tain /ˌɛntərˈteɪn/ *verb* to interest and amuse someone: *He entertained us with jokes all evening.*

en·thu·si·asm /ɛnˈθuziæzəm/ *noun* a strong feeling of excitement or interest in something: *Jan showed great enthusiasm for the new project.*

en·tire /ɪnˈtaɪər/ *adj.* (only before a noun) (used to emphasize that the whole of something is involved) including everything, everyone, or every part: *the entire world*

en·vi·ron·ment AWL /ɛnˈvaɪərnmənt/ *noun* the conditions in which you live, work, etc.: *A bad home environment can affect a child's progress in school.*

es·sen·tial /ɪˈsɛnʃl/ *adj.* completely necessary; that you must have or do: *It is absolutely essential to have a passport to travel to the U.S.*

ex·act /ɪgˈzækt/ *adj.* completely correct; accurate: *He's in his mid-fifties. Well, 56 to be exact.*

ex·ag·ger·ate /ɪgˈzædʒəreɪt/ *verb* to make something seem larger, better, worse, etc. than it really is: *Don't exaggerate. I was only two minutes late, not twenty.*

ex·pand AWL /ɪkˈspænd/ *verb*
expand on to give more details of a story, plan, idea, etc.

ex·pect /ɪkˈspɛkt/ *verb* to think or believe that someone or something will come or that something will happen: *She was expecting an e-mail from them this morning, but it didn't come.*

ex·pe·ri·ence /ɪkˈspɪriəns/ *noun* something that has happened to you, often something unusual or exciting: *She wrote a book about her experiences in Africa.*

ex·pert `AWL` /'ɛkspərt/ *noun* a person who has a lot of special knowledge or skill: *He's an expert on the history of rock music.*

ex·traor·di·nar·y /ɪk'strɔrdə,nɛri/ *adj.* unusually good, large, etc.: *She had an extraordinary ability to learn new languages.*

fac·tor `AWL` /'fæktər/ *noun* one of the things that influences a decision, situation, etc.: *His unhappiness at home was a major factor in his decision to move away.*

fa·mil·iar /fə'mɪlyər/ *adj.* well known (to someone): *It was a relief to see a familiar face in the crowd.*

fea·ture `AWL` /'fitʃər/ *noun* an important or noticeable part of something: *Lakes are a main feature of the landscape of Ontario.*

fit /fɪt/ *verb*
fit in to be able to live, work, etc. in an easy and natural way (with someone or something): *The new girl found it difficult to fit in (with the other kids) at school.*

float /floʊt/ *verb* to stay or move gently on the surface of a liquid and not sink: *Cork floats in water.*

fo·cus `AWL` /'foʊkəs/ *verb* to give all your attention to something: *to focus on a problem*

force /fɔrs/ *noun* physical strength or power: *The force of the explosion knocked them to the ground.*

for·mal /'fɔrml/ *adj.* used when you want to appear serious or official and when you are in a situation in which you do not know the other people very well: *"Yours sincerely" is a formal way of ending a letter.*

foun·da·tion `AWL` /faʊn'deɪʃn/ *noun* an organization that provides money for a special purpose, for example for research or to help people who have a particular problem: *The National Kidney Foundation (= researching the causes of kidney disease)*

func·tion `AWL` /'fʌŋkʃn/ *verb* to work correctly; to be in action: *My new computer isn't functioning very well.*

fur·ther /'fərðər/ *adj.* more; additional: *Are there any further questions?*

gath·er /'gæðər/ *verb* to bring many things together; to collect: *They have gathered together a lot of information on the subject.*

gen·er·ate `AWL` /'dʒɛnəreɪt/ *verb* to produce or create something: *I think this idea will generate a lot of interest.*

gentle /'dʒɛntəl/ *adj.* not rough or violent: *A gentle breeze was blowing through the trees.*

grant `AWL` /grænt/ *verb* to give someone what he/she has asked for: *He was granted permission to leave early.*

han·dle /'hændl/ *verb* to deal with or to control someone or something: *I have a problem at work and I don't really know how to handle it.*

high·light `AWL` /'haɪlaɪt/ *verb* to give special attention to something: *The report highlighted the need for improved safety.*

i·de·al /aɪ'diəl/ *adj.* the best possible: *In an ideal world, there would be no poverty.*

i·den·ti·fy `AWL` /aɪ'dɛntəfaɪ/ *verb* to recognize or be able to say who or what someone or something is: *The police need someone to identify the body.*

im·age `AWL` /'ɪmɪdʒ/ *noun* a mental picture or idea of someone or something: *I have an image of my childhood as always warm and sunny.*

i·mag·i·na·tion /ɪ,mædʒə'neɪʃn/ *noun* the ability to create mental pictures or new ideas: *He has a lively imagination.*

im·me·di·ate /ɪ'midiət/ *adj.* happening or done without delay: *I'd like an immediate answer to my proposal.*

im·pact /'ɪmpækt/ *noun* an effect or impression: *Her speech made a great impact on the audience.*

im·prove /ɪm'pruv/ *verb* to become or to make something better: *I hope the weather will improve later on.*

in·clude /ɪn'klud/ *verb* to have as one part; to contain (among other things): *The price of the room includes one drink in the hotel bar.*

in·di·vid·u·al /,ɪndə'vɪdʒuəl/ *adj.* (only before a noun) single or particular: *Each individual battery is tested before being packaged.*

in·form /ɪnˈfɔrm/ *verb* to give someone information (about something): *You should inform the police about the accident.*

in·i·tia·tive /ɪˈnɪʃətɪv/ *noun* official action that is taken to solve a problem or improve a situation: *a new government initiative to help people start small businesses*

in·tend /ɪnˈtɛnd/ *verb* to plan or mean to do something: *I spent more money than I had intended.*

in·ter·rupt /ˌɪntəˈrʌpt/ *verb* to say or do something that makes someone stop what he/she is saying or doing: *I'm sorry to interrupt, but there's a phone call for you.*

is·sue /ˈɪʃu/ *noun* a problem or subject for discussion: *The government cannot avoid the issue of homelessness any longer.*

key /ki/ *adj.* very important: *Tourism is a key industry in Florida.*

knowl·edge /ˈnɑlɪdʒ/ *noun* information or facts that you have in your mind about something: *He has extensive knowledge of ancient Egypt.*

land·scape /ˈlænskeɪp/ *noun* everything you can see when you look across a large area of land: *The prairie landscape is very flat.*

lim·it /ˈlɪmət/ *noun* a point or line that marks the end or edge of something: *No alcohol is sold within the city limits* (=inside the city).

link AWL /lɪŋk/ *noun* a person or thing that connects two other people or things: *There is a strong link between smoking and heart disease.*

lo·cal /ˈloʊkl/ *adj.* of or in a particular place (near you): *local newspapers*

lo·ca·tion AWL /loʊˈkeɪʃn/ *noun* a place or position: *Several locations have been suggested for the new stadium.*

man·age /ˈmænɪdʒ/ *verb* to succeed in doing or dealing with something difficult; to be able to do something: *I'm sorry I didn't manage to write that report last week.*

mass /mæs/ *noun* a large amount or number of something: *The garden was a mass of flowers.*

mat·ter /ˈmæt̮ər/ *noun* a subject or situation that you must think about and give your attention to: *It's a personal matter and I don't want to discuss it with you.*

mem·o·ry /ˈmɛməri/ *noun* something that you remember: *That is one of my happiest memories.*

men·tion /ˈmɛnʃn/ *verb* to say or write something about someone or something; to talk about someone or something: *I wouldn't mention her exams to her— she's feeling nervous.*

meth·od AWL /ˈmɛθəd/ *noun* a way of doing something: *modern methods of teaching languages*

mi·nor·i·ty AWL /məˈnɔrət̮i; maɪ-; -ˈnɑr-/ *noun* the smaller number or part of a group; less than half: *Most women continue to work when they are married. Only a minority stays/stay at home.*

mon·i·tor AWL /ˈmɑnət̮ər/ *noun* a machine, often a part of a computer, that shows information or pictures on a screen like a television

mood /mud/ *noun* the way that a group of people feel about something: *The mood of the meeting was very optimistic.*

net·work AWL /ˈnɛtwərk/ *noun* a system of computers that are connected by cables or telephone lines

nor·mal AWL /ˈnɔrml/ *adj.* (used about a person or animal) formed or developed in the usual way: *The child was completely normal at birth.*

note /noʊt/ *verb* to mention something: *I'd like to note that the project has been extremely successful so far.*

no·tice /ˈnoʊt̮əs/ *verb* to see and be aware of something: *"What kind of car was the man driving?" "I didn't notice."*

ob·jec·tive AWL /əbˈdʒɛktɪv/ *noun* your aim or purpose: *Our objective is to finish by the end of the year.*

ob·vi·ous AWL /ˈɑbviəs/ *adj.* easily seen or understood; clear: *It was obvious that he was not well.*

oc·cur `AWL` /ə'kər/ *verb* to come into someone's mind: *It never occurred to John that his wife might be unhappy.*

odd /ɑd/ *adj.* strange; unusual: *There's something odd about him.*

op·er·ate /'ɑpəreɪt/ *verb* to do business; to manage or direct something: *The corporation operates from its headquarters in Atlanta.*

op·por·tu·ni·ty /ˌɑpər'tunət̬i/ *noun* a chance to do something that you would like to do; a situation or a time in which it is possible to do something: *The trip gave me a great opportunity to use my Spanish.*

or·gan·ize /'ɔrgənaɪz/ *verb* to put things into order; to arrange into a system or logical order: *Can you decide what needs to be done? I'm terrible at organizing.*

o·rig·i·nal /ə'rɪdʒənl/ *adj.* first; earliest (before changes or developments): *The original meaning of this word is different from the meaning it has nowadays.*

or·i·gin /'ɔrədʒɪn; 'ɑr-/ *noun* the time when or place where something first comes into existence; the reason why something starts: *Could you explain the origins of this tradition to me?*

pace /peɪs/ *noun* the speed at which you do something or at which something happens: *Run at a steady pace and you won't get tired so quickly.*

par·tic·u·lar /pər'tɪkyələr/ *adj.* (only before a noun) more than usual; special: *This article is of particular interest to me.*

pa·tience /'peɪʃns/ *noun* the quality of being able to remain calm and not get angry, especially when there is a difficulty or you have to wait a long time: *I have no patience with people who don't even try.*

pat·tern /'pæt̬ərn/ *noun* the way in which something happens, develops, or is done: *Her days all seemed to follow the same pattern.*

pause /pɔz/ *noun* a short period of time during which something stops: *He continued playing for twenty minutes without a pause.*

per·form·ance /pər'fɔrməns/ *noun* how well or badly you do something; how well or badly something works: *The company's performance was disappointing last year.*

per·mit /pər'mɪt/ *verb* to allow something: *Food and drink are not permitted in this building.*

per·suade /pər'sweɪd/ *verb* to make someone believe something: *The attorney persuaded the jury that she was innocent.*

po·ten·tial `AWL` /pə'tɛnʃl/ *noun* the qualities or abilities that someone or something has but that may not be fully developed yet: *That boy has great potential as a pianist.*

pre·cise `AWL` /prɪ'saɪs/ *adj.* (only before a noun) exact; particular: *It is difficult to determine the precise moment when the crime occurred.*

pres·sure /'prɛʃər/ *noun* a situation that causes you to be worried or unhappy: *They moved to the suburbs to escape the pressure of city life.*

pre·tend /prɪ'tɛnd/ *verb* to behave in a particular way in order to make other people believe something that is not true: *Frances walked past, pretending (that) she didn't see me.*

pre·vent /prɪ'vɛnt/ *verb* to stop something from happening or to stop someone from doing something: *Everyone hopes the negotiations will prevent a war.*

pre·vi·ous `AWL` /'priviəs/ *adj.* coming or happening before or earlier: *Do you have previous experience in this type of work?*

prin·ci·ple `AWL` /'prɪnsəpl/ *noun* a basic general rule or truth about something: *We believe in the principle of equal opportunity for everyone.*

pro·ceed `AWL` /prə'sid; proʊ-/ *verb* to go on to do something else: *After getting an estimate, we can decide whether or not to proceed with the work.*

pro·duce /prə'dus/ *verb* to cause to happen: *Her remarks produced roars of laughter.*

pro·gram /'proʊɡræm; -ɡrəm/ *verb* to make a piece of equipment work or act automatically in a particular way: *The lights are programmed to come on as soon as it gets dark.*

pro·gress /'prɑɡrɛs; -ɡrəs/ *noun* change or improvement in society: *People who oppose new technologies are accused of holding back progress.*

prop·er /'prɑpər/ *adj.* (only before a noun) right or correct: *information on the proper use of chemicals*

pro·por·tion AWL /prə'pɔrʃn/ *noun* a part or share of a whole: *A large proportion of the earth's surface is covered by oceans.*

pure /pyʊr/ *adj.* (old-fashioned) not doing or knowing anything evil: *to remain spiritually pure*

qual·i·fi·ca·tion /ˌkwɑləfə'keɪʃn/ *noun* a skill or quality that makes you suitable to do something, such as a job: *She has all the right qualifications for the manager's job.*

rap·id /'ræpəd/ *adj.* happening very quickly or moving with great speed: *She made rapid progress and was soon the best in the class.*

reach /ritʃ/ *verb* to arrive at a place or condition: *We won't reach the airport in time.*

re·ac·tion AWL /ri'ækʃn/ *noun* something that you do or say because of something that has happened or been said: *What is your reaction to the news?*

re·al·i·ty /ri'æləti/ *noun* something that really exists, not something that is imagined: *Death is a reality that everyone has to face eventually.*

re·al·ize /'riəlaɪz/ *verb* to become aware of something or that something has happened, usually some time later: *When I got home, I realized that I had left my keys at the office.*

rea·son·a·ble /'rizn·əbl/ *adj.* acceptable and appropriate in a particular situation: *That seems like a reasonable decision under the circumstances.*

re·call /rɪ'kɔl/ *verb* to remember something (a fact, event, action, etc.) from the past: *I don't recall exactly when I first met her.*

rec·og·nize /'rɛkəɡnaɪz/ *verb* to know again someone or something that you have seen or heard before: *I recognized him, but I couldn't remember his name.*

re·fer /rɪ'fər/ *verb* to be used to describe someone or something: *The term "adolescent" refers to young people between the ages of 13 and 17.*

re·gion /'ridʒən/ *noun* a part of the country or the world; a large area of land: *This region of the country is very flat.*

reg·is·ter AWL /'rɛdʒəstər/ *verb* to show feelings, opinions, etc.: *Her face registered intense dislike.*

re·late /rɪ'leɪt/ *verb* to show a connection between two or more things: *The report relates heart disease to high levels of stress.*

re·la·tion·ship /rɪ'leɪʃnʃɪp/ *noun* the way that people, groups, countries, etc. feel about or behave toward each other: *The police have a poor relationship with the local people.*

rel·e·vant AWL /'rɛləvənt/ *adj.* connected with what is happening or being talked about: *Please enclose all the relevant documents with your visa application.*

re·ly AWL /rɪ'laɪ/ *verb* to need someone or something and not be able to live or work well without him/her/it: *The old lady had to rely on other people to go shopping for her.*

re·main /rɪ'meɪn/ *verb* to stay or continue in the same place or condition: *They remained silent throughout the trial.*

re·mark·a·ble /rɪ'mɑrkəbl/ *adj.* unusual and surprising in a way that people notice: *She certainly is a remarkable woman.*

re·quire AWL /rɪ'kwaɪər/ *verb* to need something: *Please contact us if you require further information.*

re·source AWL /'risɔrs; rɪ'sɔrs/ *noun* a supply of something, a piece of equipment, etc. that is available for someone to use: *The video is an excellent resource for teachers.*

re·sponse AWL /rɪ'spɑns/ *noun* an answer or reaction to someone or something: *I've sent my résumé to 20 companies, but I haven't received any responses yet.*

re·spon·si·bil·i·ty /rɪˌspɑnsəˈbɪləti/ *noun* a duty to deal with something so that it is your fault if something goes wrong: *It is John's responsibility to make sure the orders are sent out on time.*

re·veal **AWL** /rɪˈvil/ *verb* to show something that was hidden before: *Close inspection of the photograph revealed the identity of the gunman.*

sad·ness /ˈsædnəs/ *noun* the feeling of being sad: *I felt a deep sadness.*

sat·is·fac·tion /ˌsætəsˈfækʃn/ *noun* a feeling of pleasure that you have when you have done, gotten, or achieved what you wanted: *Gwen stood back and looked at her work with a sense of satisfaction.*

sat·is·fy /ˈsætəsfaɪ/ *verb* to make someone pleased by doing or giving him/her what he/she wants: *Nothing satisfies him—he's always complaining.*

sen·si·ble /ˈsɛnsəbl/ *adj.* having or showing the ability to think or act in a reasonable way; having or showing good judgment: *It was a realistic and sensible plan.*

share /ʃɛr/ *verb* to tell someone about something; to allow someone to know something: *Sometimes it helps to share your problems.*

shel·ter /ˈʃɛltər/ *verb* to protect someone or something; to give someone or something shelter: *The trees shelter the house from the wind.*

shift **AWL** /ʃɪft/ *noun* (in a factory, etc.) a division of the working day; the people who work during this period: *an eight-hour shift*

show /ʃoʊ/ *verb* **show off** to try to impress people by showing them how good you are at something or by showing them something that you are proud of: *He's always showing off in front of his friends.*

sig·nal /ˈsɪɡnəl/ *verb* to make a signal; to send a particular message using a signal: *He signaled his disapproval by leaving the room.*

sig·nif·i·cant **AWL** /sɪɡˈnɪfəkənt/ *adj.* important or large enough to be noticed: *There has been a significant increase in the number of crimes reported this year.*

sim·ple /ˈsɪmpl/ *adj.* easy to understand, do, or use; not difficult or complicated: *This dictionary is written in simple English.*

sim·plic·i·ty /sɪmˈplɪsəti/ *noun* the quality of being easy to understand, do, or use: *We all admired the simplicity of the plan.*

source **AWL** /sɔrs/ *noun* a place, person, or thing where something comes or starts from or where something is obtained: *Sales tax is an important source of income for the government.*

space /speɪs/ *noun* an area that is empty or not used: *Is there enough space for me to park the car there?*

spe·cif·ics **AWL** /spəˈsɪfɪks/ *noun* the details of a subject that you need to think about or discuss: *Okay, that's the broad plan—let's get down to the specifics.*

spir·it /ˈspɪrɪt/ *noun* a strong feeling of being loyal to a group, an organization, etc. and of wanting to help it: *fun activities to build school spirit*

spoil /spɔɪl/ *verb* to do too much for someone, especially a child, so that you have a bad effect on his/her character: *His grandmother spoils him by buying him all the candy he wants.*

stand /stænd/ *verb* **stand out** to be easily seen or noticed

stan·dard /ˈstændərd/ *noun* a level of quality: *We need to improve educational standards in this state.*

strat·e·gy **AWL** /ˈstrætədʒi/ *noun* a plan that you use in order to achieve something: *a strategy to reduce inflation*

style **AWL** /staɪl/ *noun* the way that someone usually writes, behaves, etc.: *Hemingway's style is very clear and simple.*

suc·cess /səkˈsɛs/ *noun* the fact that you have achieved what you want; doing well and becoming famous, rich, etc.: *Hard work is the key to success.*

suf·fi·cient **AWL** /səˈfɪʃnt/ *adj.* as much as is necessary; enough: *We have sufficient oil reserves to last for three months.*

sug·gest /səɡˈdʒɛst; səˈdʒɛ-/ *verb* to propose a plan or idea for someone to discuss or consider: *Can anyone suggest ways of raising more money?*

suit·a·ble /ˈsuṭəbl/ *adj.* right or convenient for someone or something: *Is this a suitable time to have a meeting?*

sup·port /səˈpɔrt/ *verb* to agree with the aims of someone or something or with an idea, a plan, etc., and to give him/her/it help, money, etc.: *I'll support you as much as I can.*

switch /swɪtʃ/ *verb* to change or be changed from one thing to another: *We've switched from eating fried foods to more fresh fruit and vegetables.*

sys·tem /ˈsɪstəm/ *noun* a group of things or parts that work together: *The whole computer system crashed.*

talk /tɔk/ *verb*
talk down to talk to someone as if he/she is less intelligent, important, etc. than you

task **AWL** /tæsk/ *noun* a piece of work that has to be done, especially an unpleasant or difficult one: *Your first task will be to send these letters.*

tech·nique **AWL** /tɛkˈnik/ *noun* a particular way of doing something: *new techniques for teaching languages*

tend /tɛnd/ *verb* to usually do or be something: *Women tend to live longer than men.*

ten·sion **AWL** /ˈtɛnʃn/ *noun* a feeling of anxiety and stress that makes it impossible to relax: *I could hear the tension in her voice as she spoke.*

the·o·ry **AWL** /ˈθɪri; ˈθiəri/ *noun* an idea or set of ideas that try to explain something: *the theory about how life on earth began*

top /tɑp/ *adj.* (only before a noun) highest in position, rank, or degree: *one of the country's top business executives*

tra·di·tion **AWL** /trəˈdɪʃn/ *noun* a custom or belief that has continued from the past to the present: *It's a tradition to play tricks on people on April 1st.*

train /treɪn/ *verb* to teach a person or an animal to do something which is difficult or which needs practice: *The organization trains guide dogs for the blind.*

val·u·a·ble /ˈvælyəbl; -yuəbl/ *adj.* very useful: *a valuable piece of information*

val·ue /ˈvælyu/ *verb* to think someone or something is very important and worth a lot: *Laura has always valued her independence.*

va·ri·e·ty /vəˈraɪəṭi/ *noun* a number of different kinds of things: *You can take evening classes in a variety of subjects including photography, Spanish, and computers.*

vast /væst/ *adj.* extremely big: *The vast majority of (=almost all) local residents support the proposal.*

view /vyu/ *noun* an opinion or idea about something: *He expressed the view that standards were falling.*

waste /weɪst/ *verb* to use or spend something in a careless way or for something that is not necessary: *He wasted his time at college because he didn't work hard.*

weak·ness /ˈwiknəs/ *noun* a fault or lack of strength, especially in a person's character: *It's important to know your own strengths and weaknesses.*